Tulips belong to the genus Tulipa.

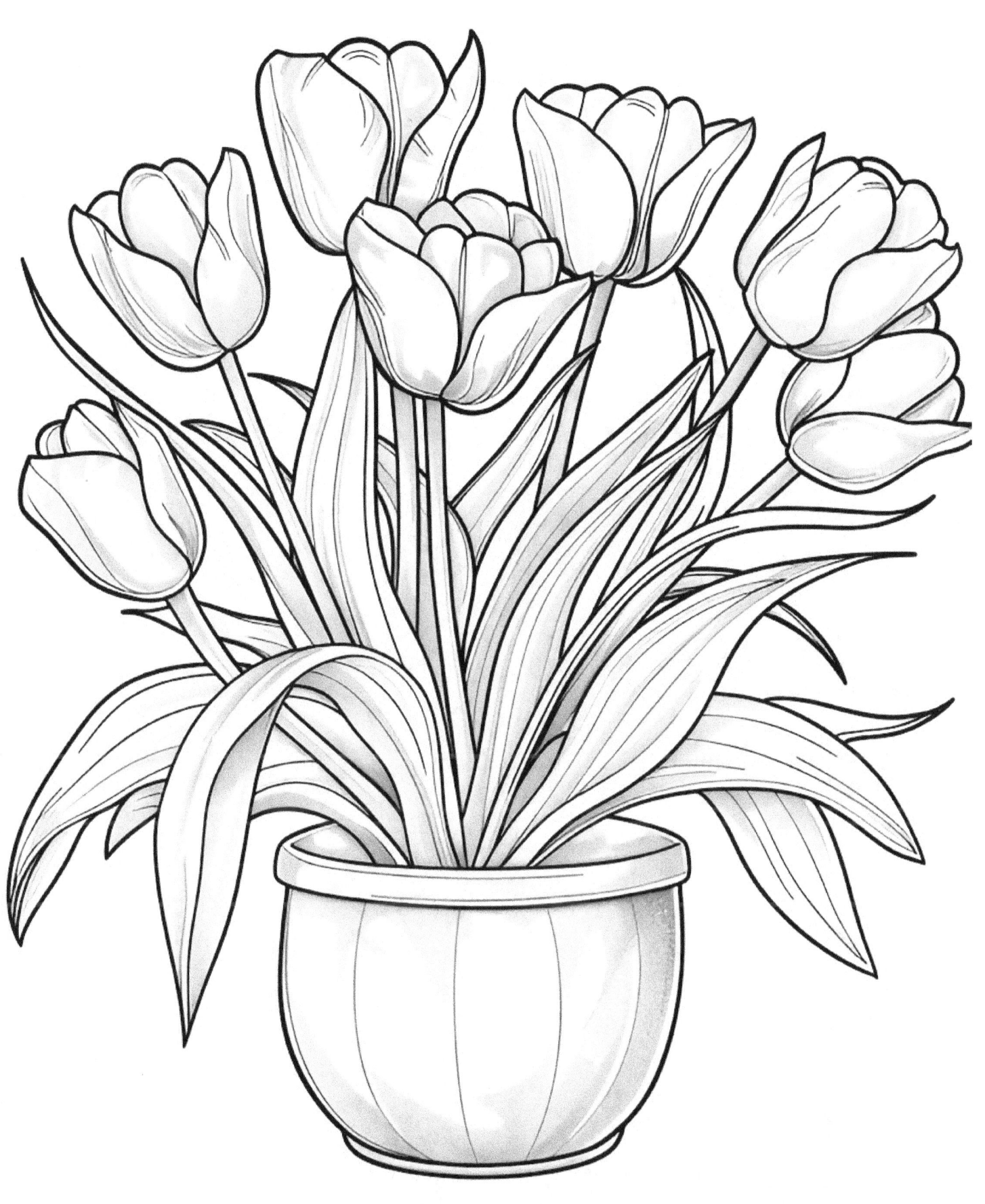

They are native to
Central Asia and
Turkey.

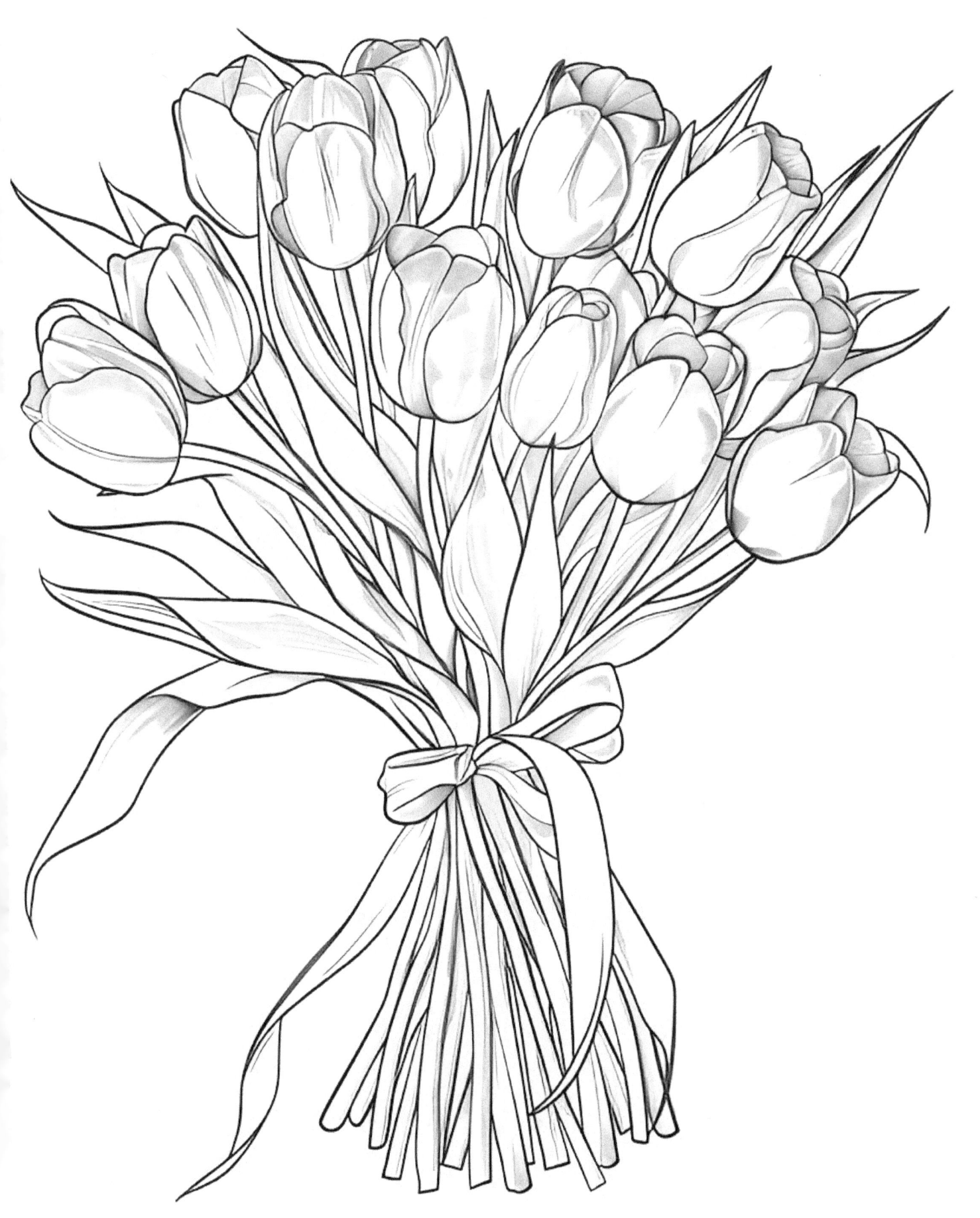

Tulips are part of the lily family, Liliaceae.

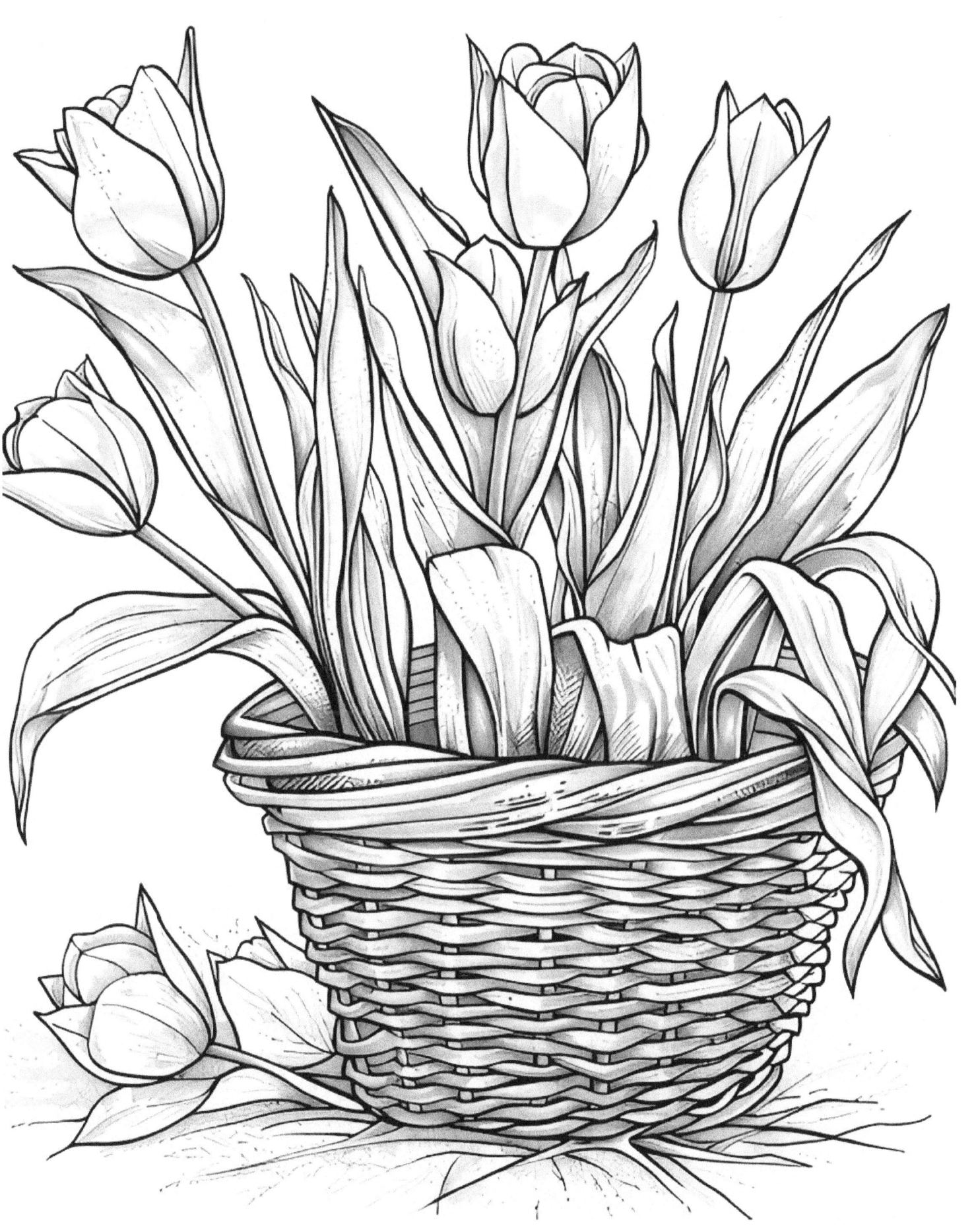

The Netherlands is famous for its tulip cultivation.

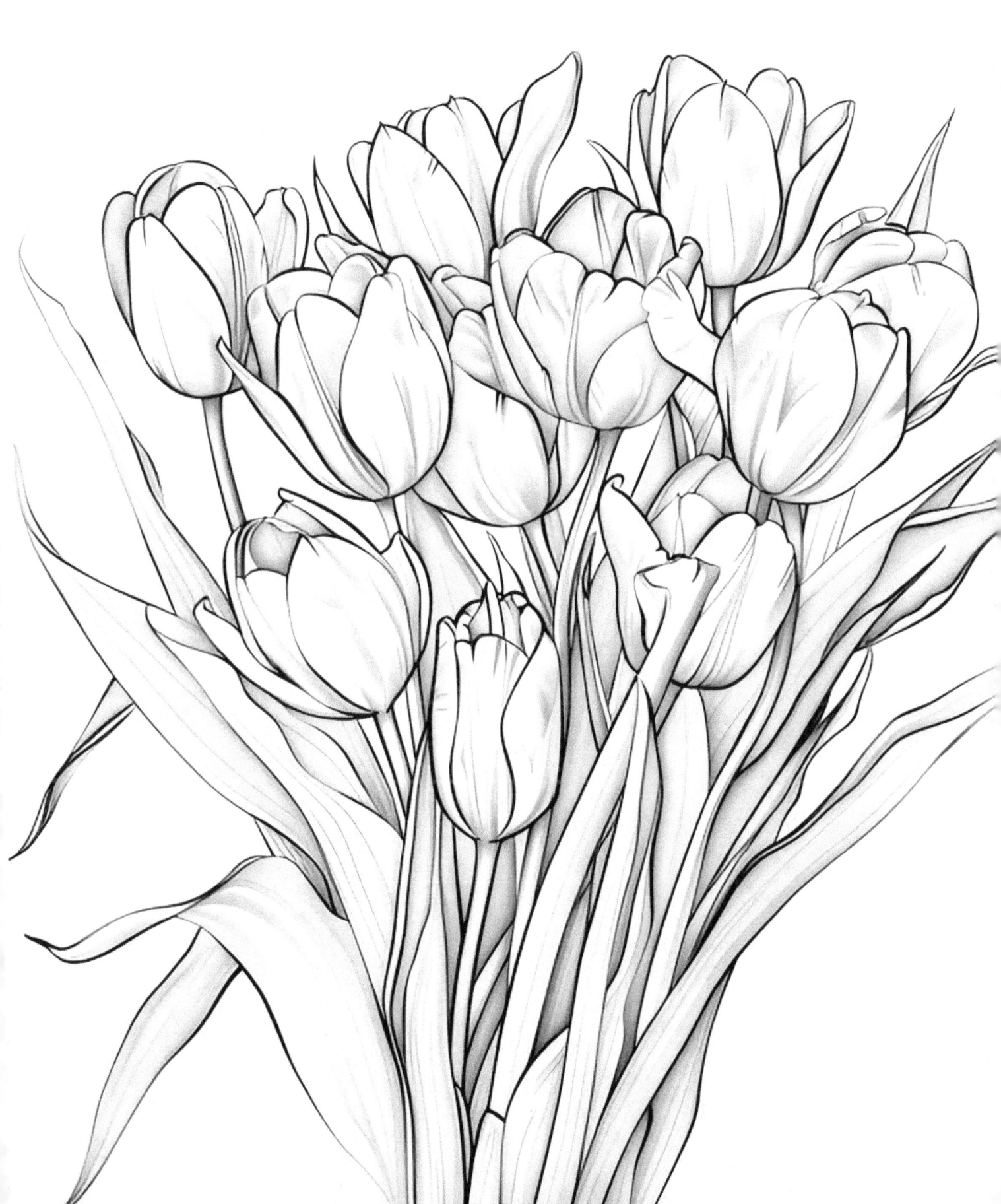

Tulips are perennial plants that grow from bulbs.

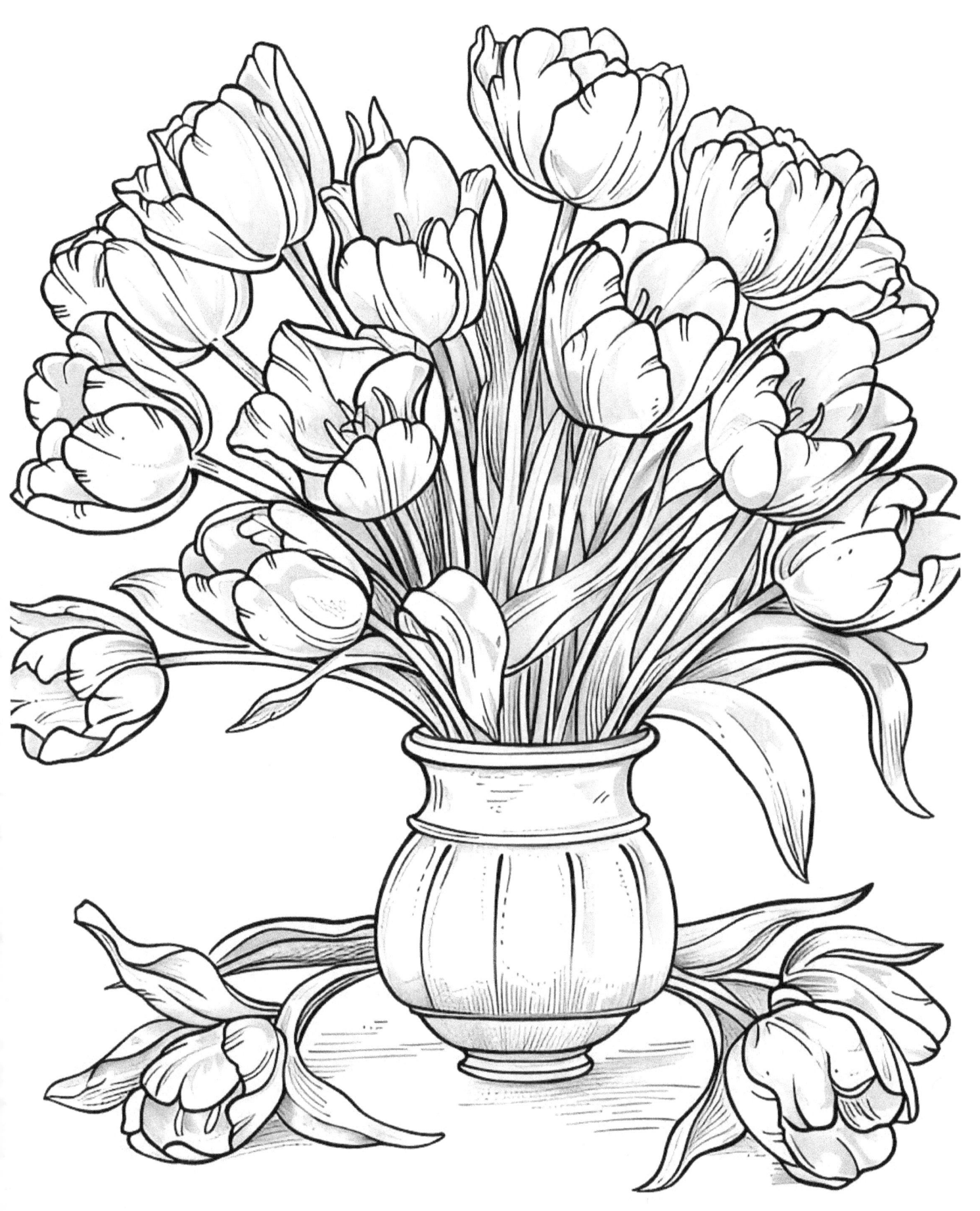

They are known for their vibrant and diverse colors.

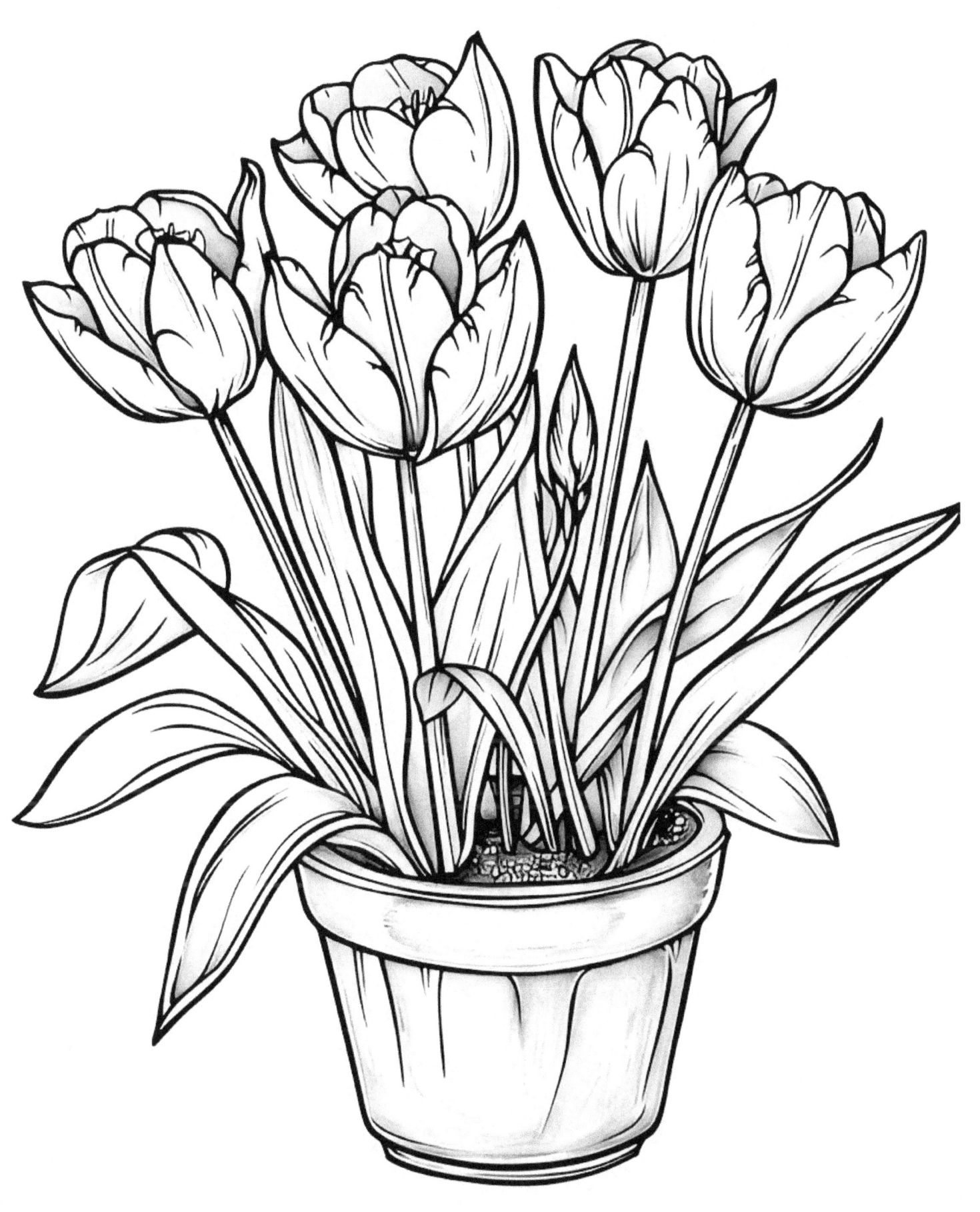

Tulips were introduced to Europe in the 16th century.

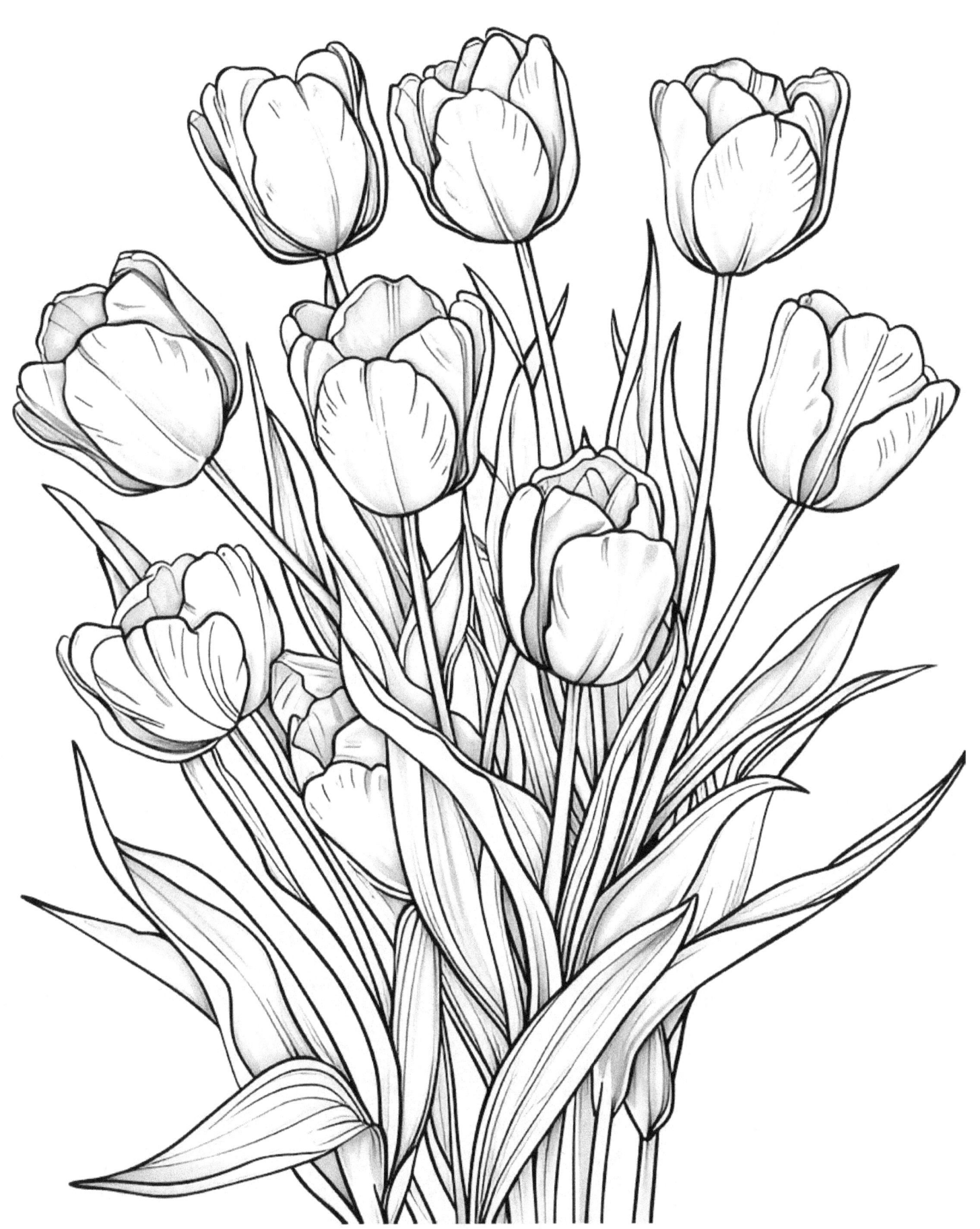

The tulip is the national flower of Turkey.

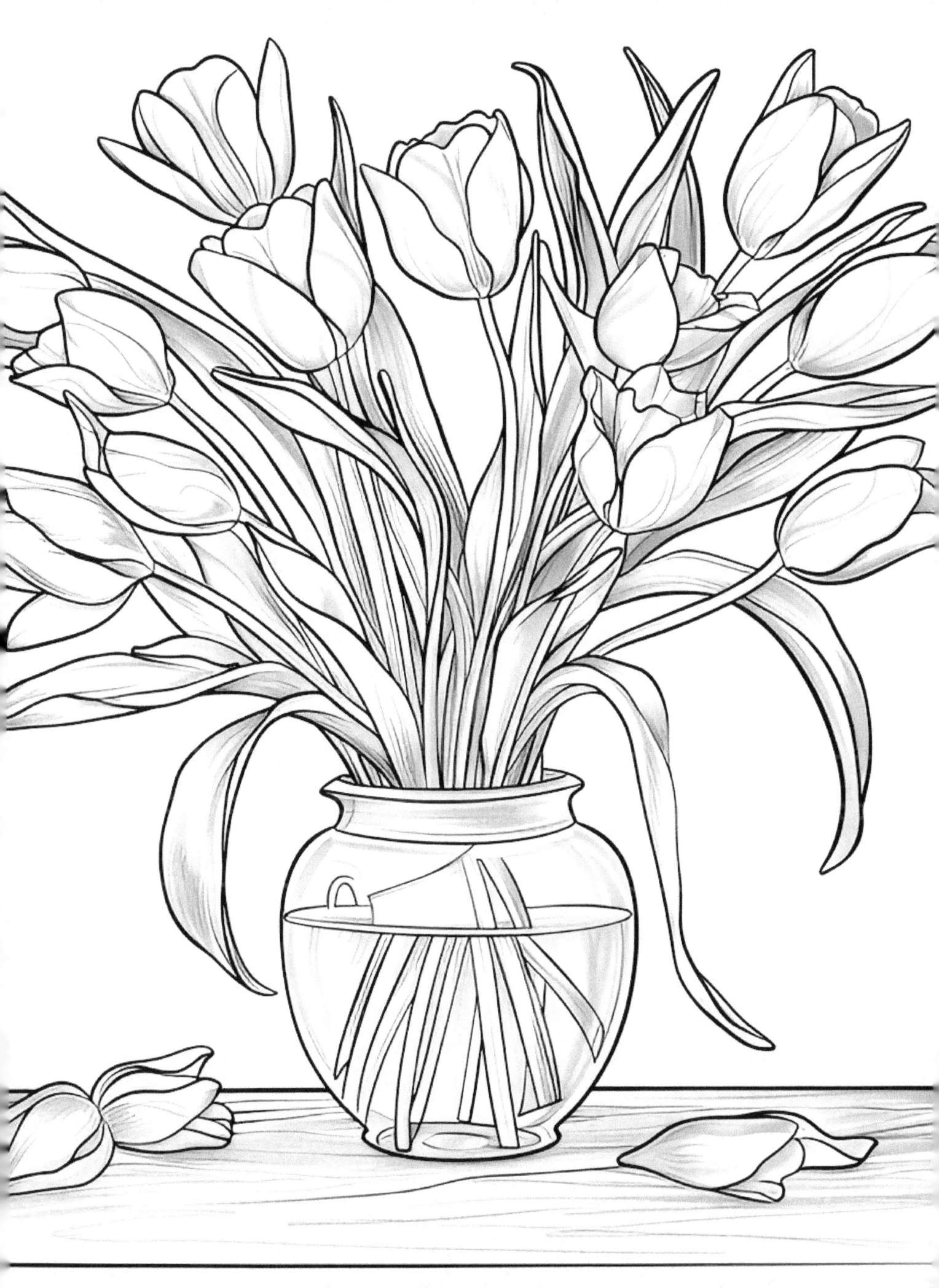

Tulips have cup-shaped flowers with six petals.

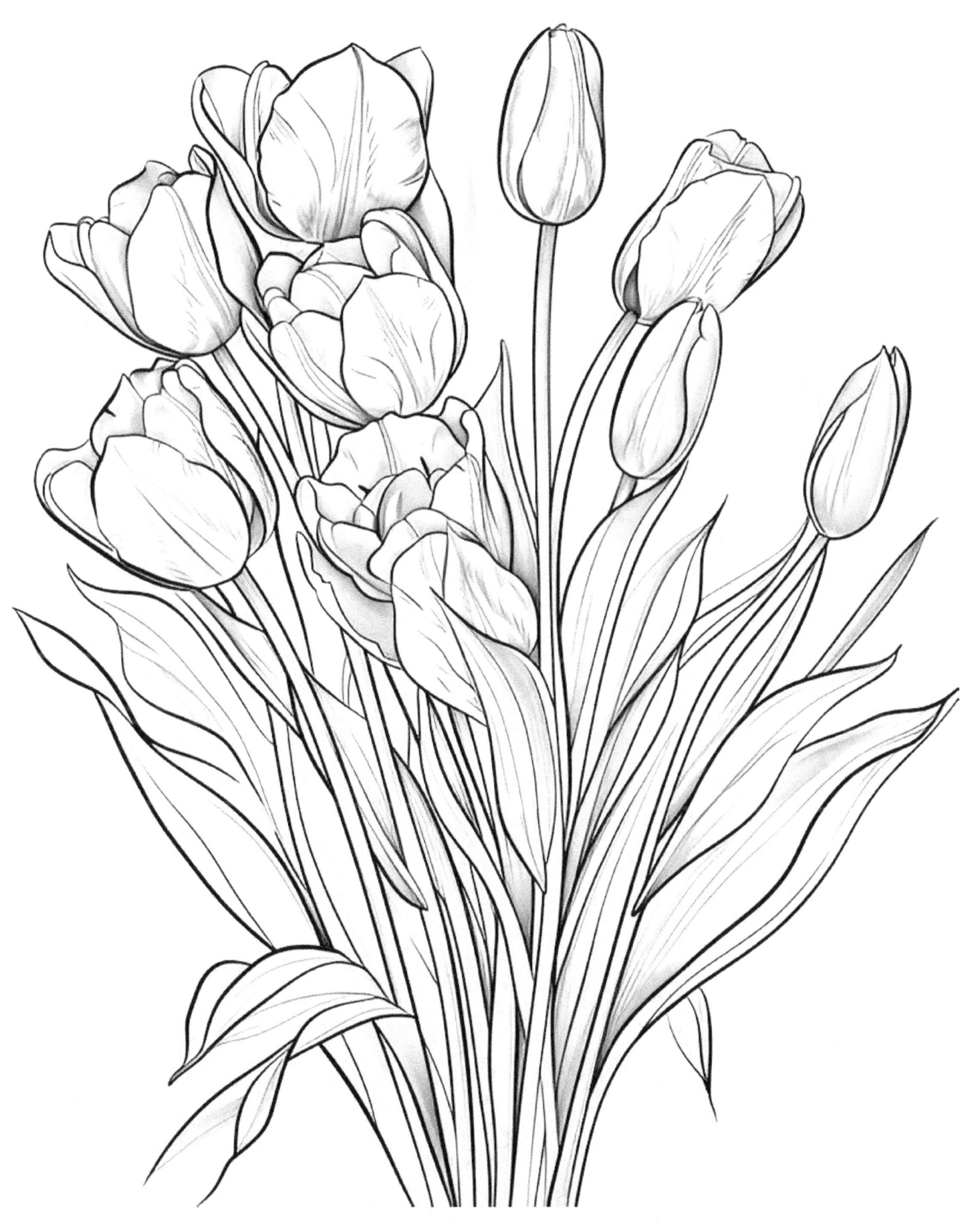

They bloom in spring, typically from March to May.

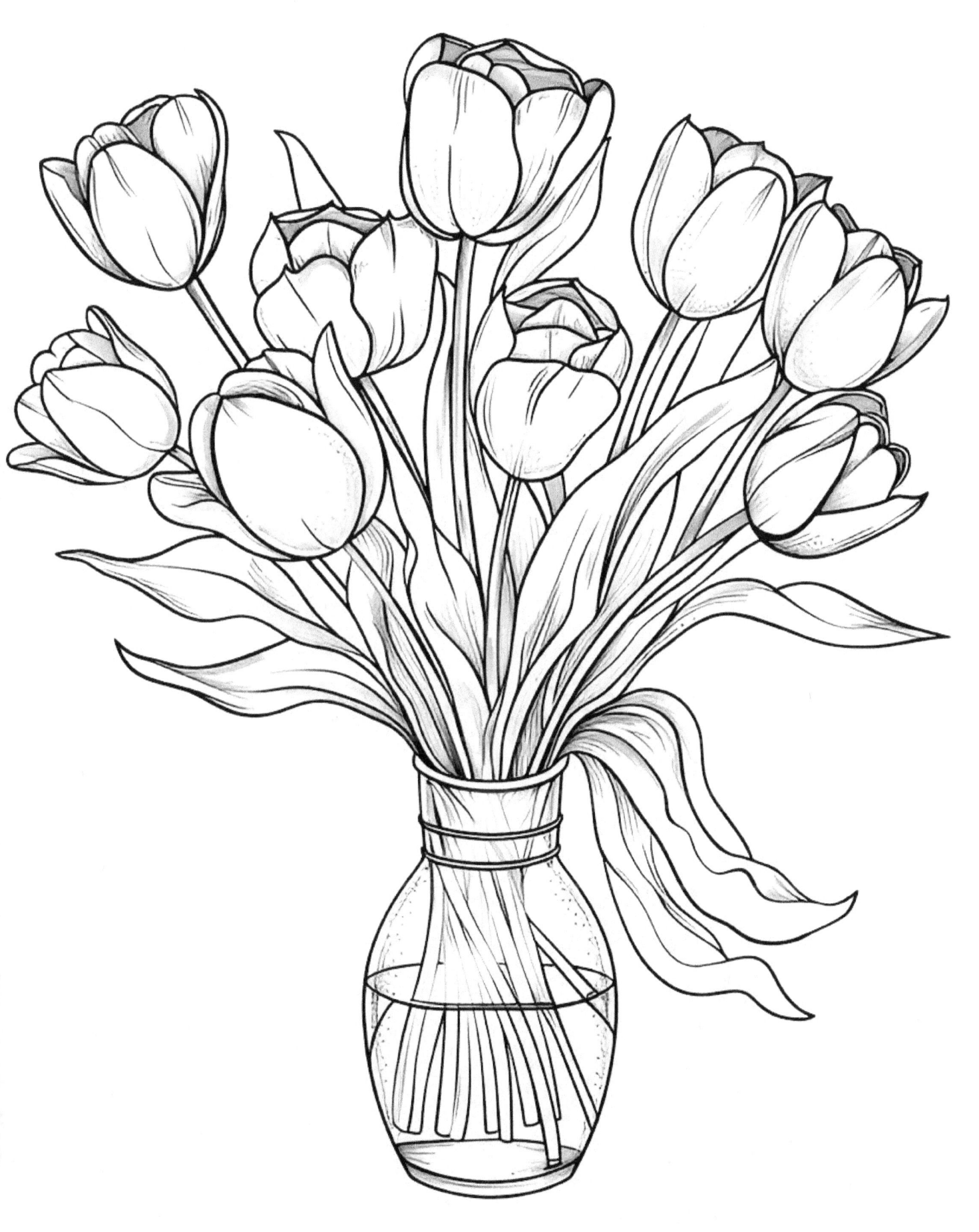

Tulips come in various shapes, including single, double, fringed and parrot.

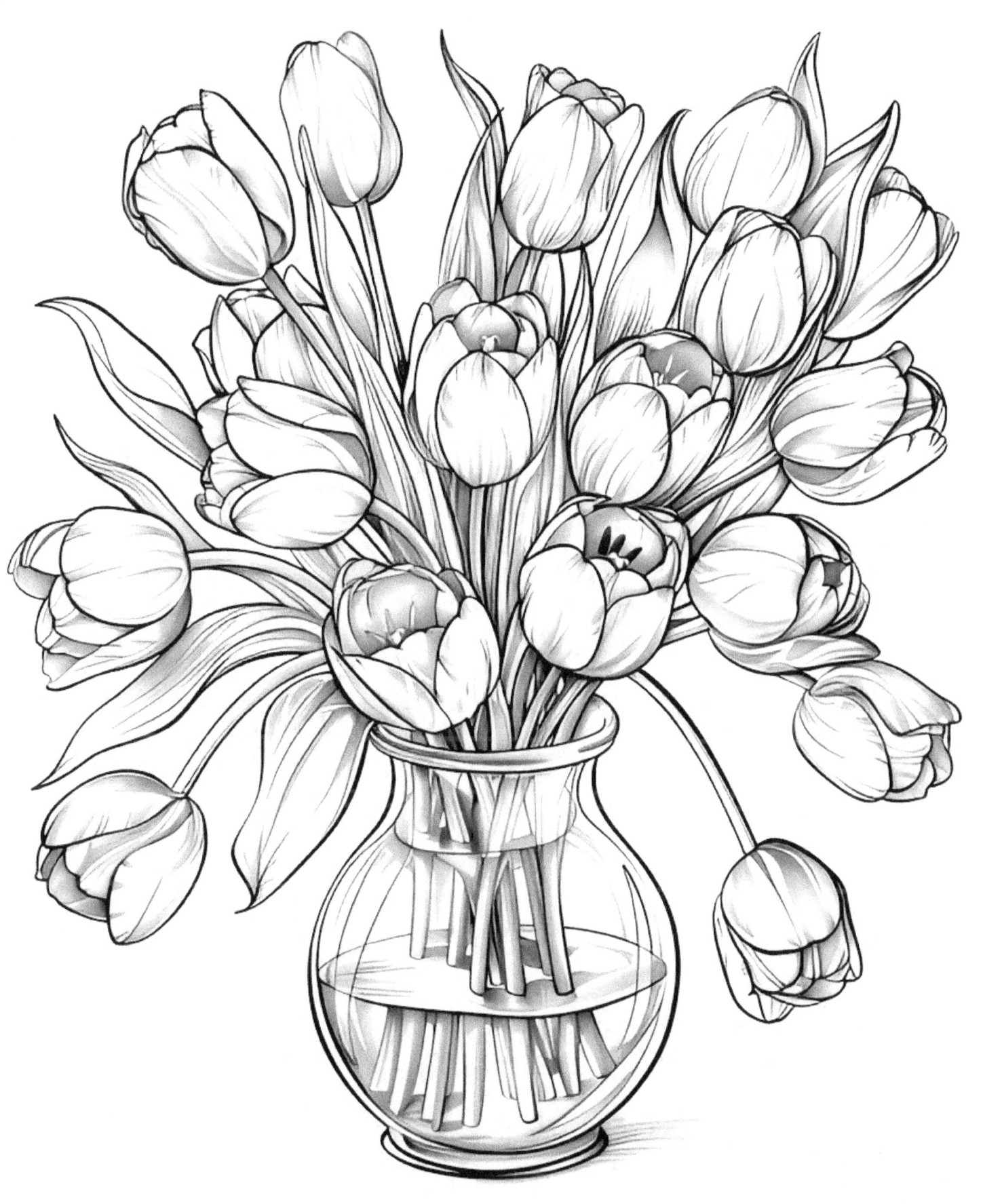

Tulips were once more valuable than gold in the Netherlands during the 17th century.

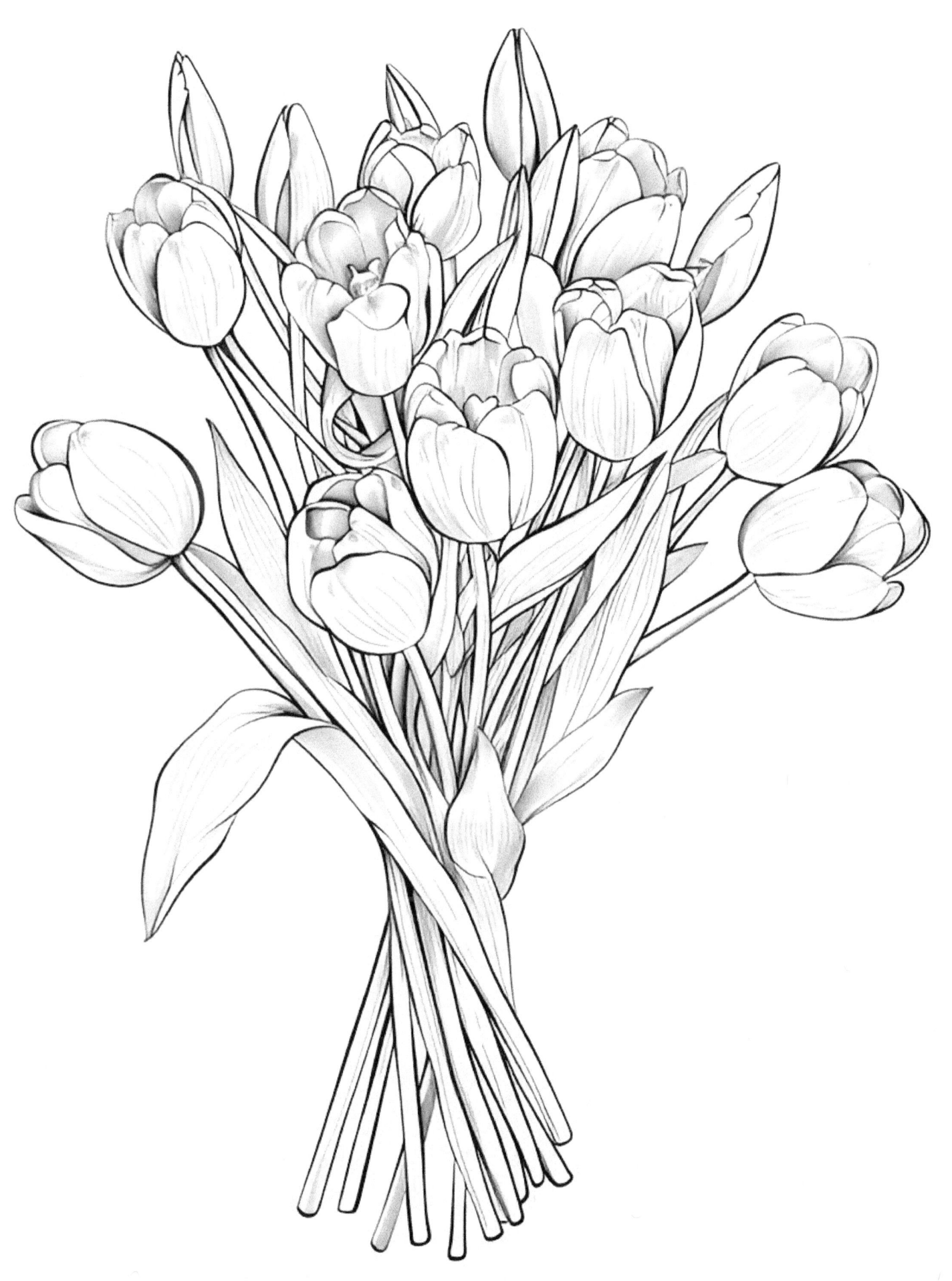

There are over 3,000 registered varieties of tulips.

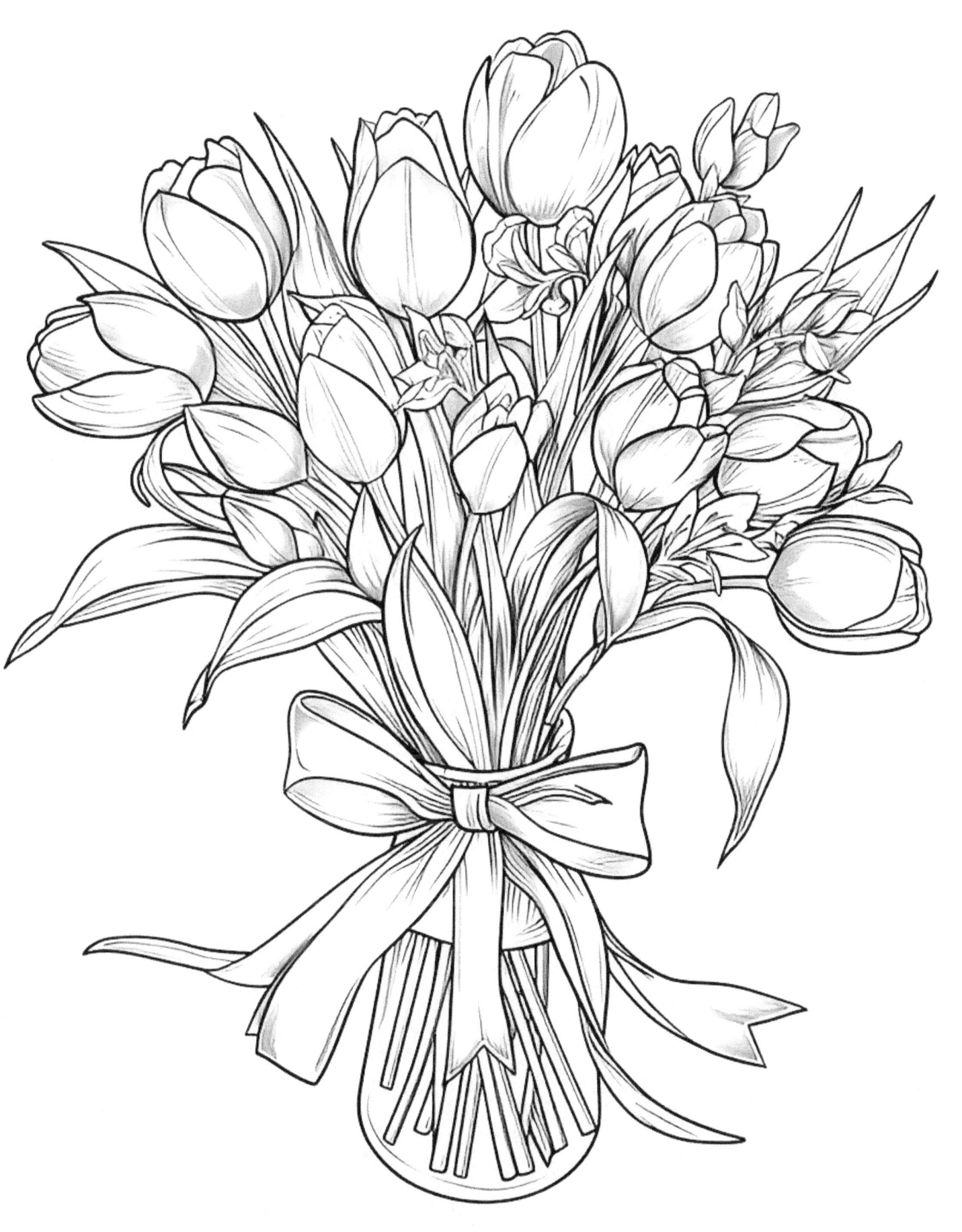

Tulips are often used in floral arrangements and bouquets.

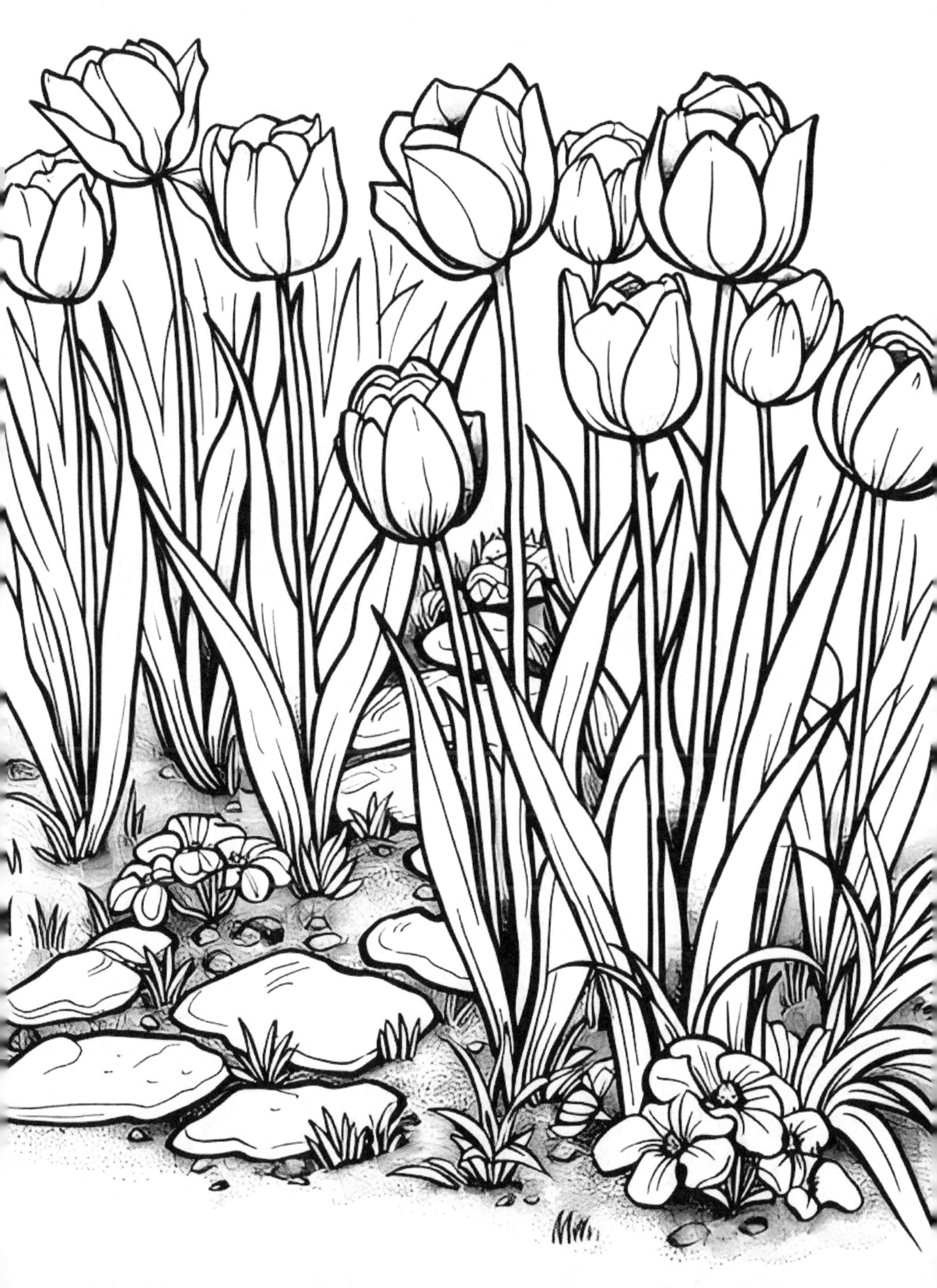

Tulip bulbs can be eaten and were consumed during times of famine.

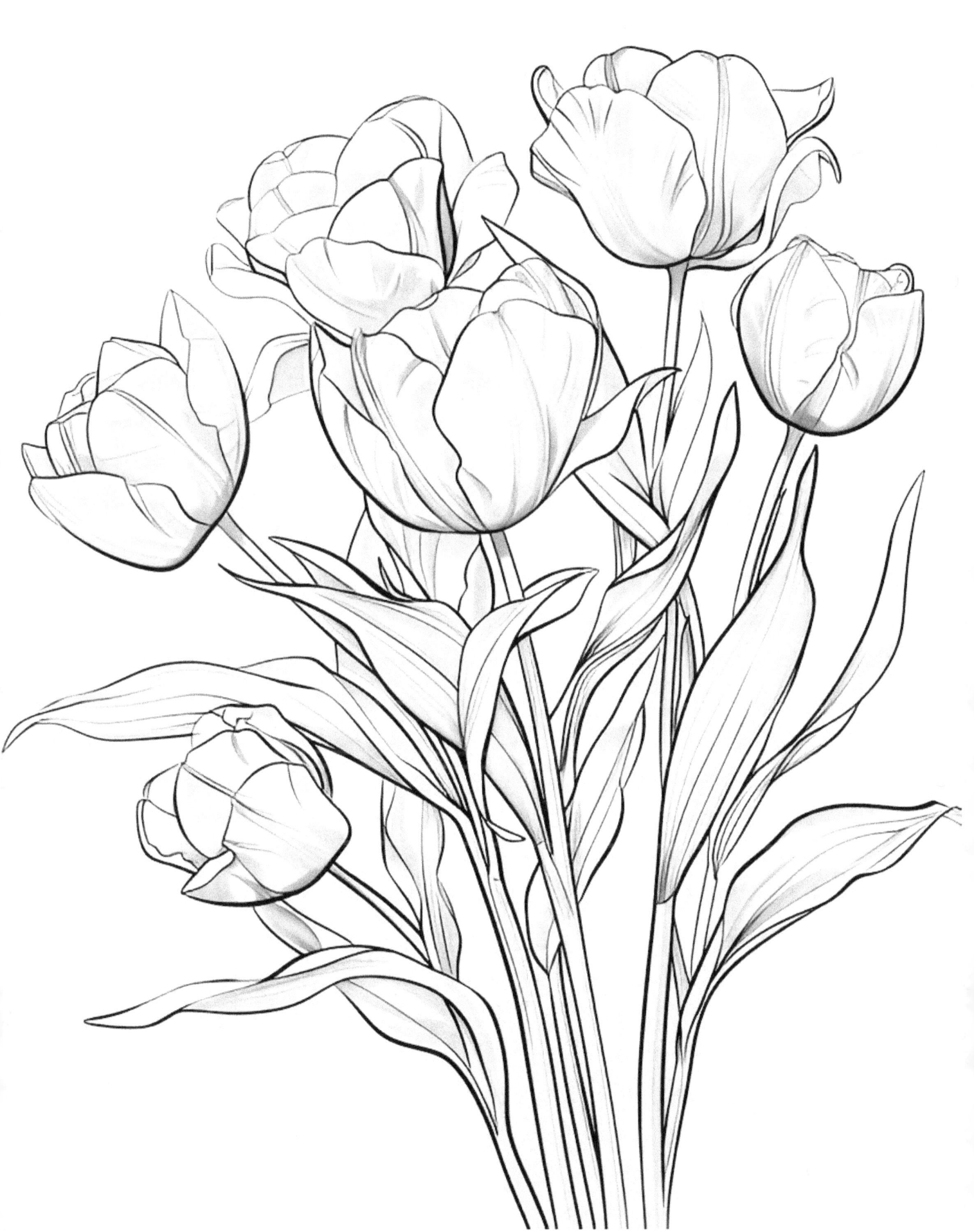

Tulips were the subjects of a speculative frenzy known as "tulip mania" in the 17th century.

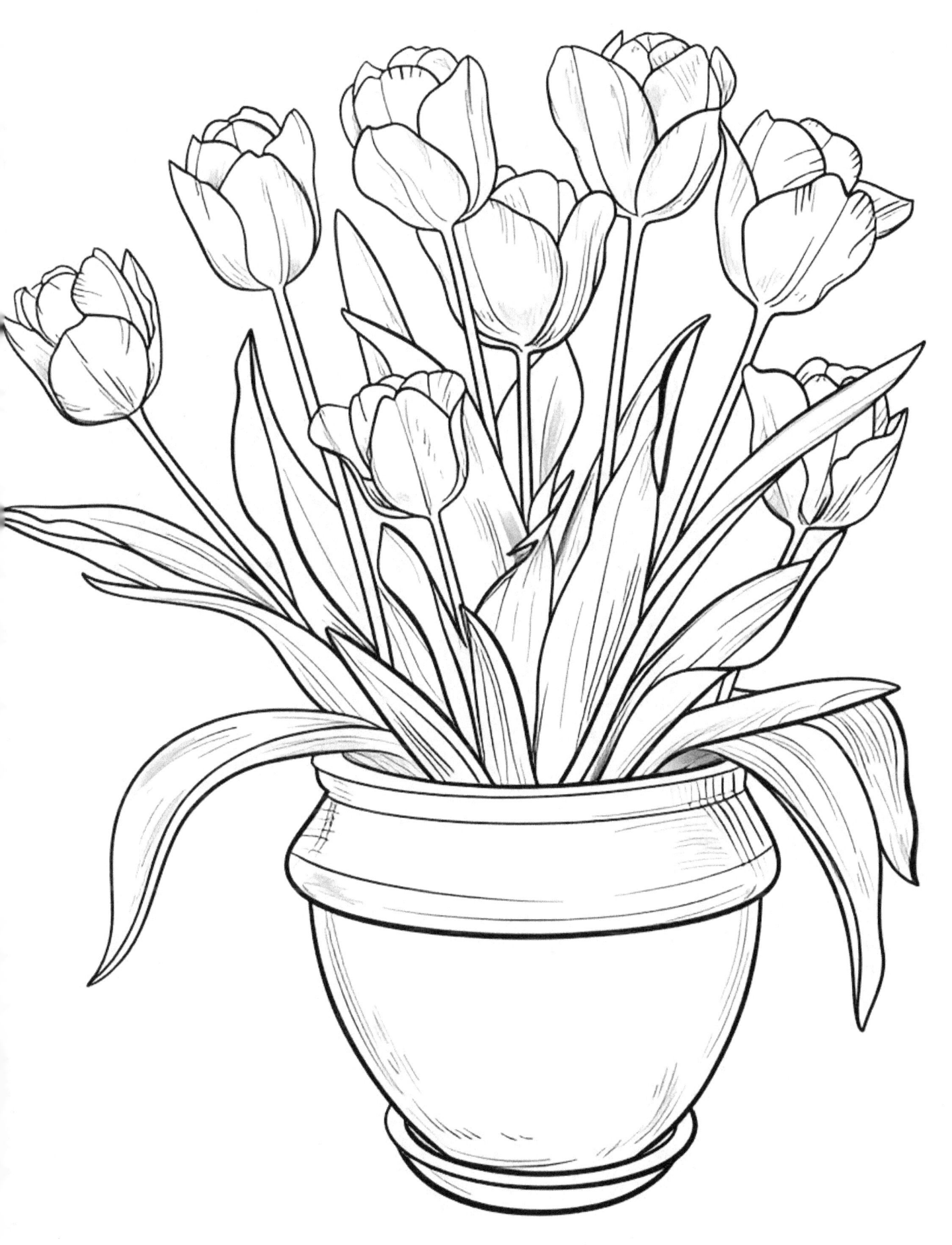

The tulip is the national flower of Afghanistan.

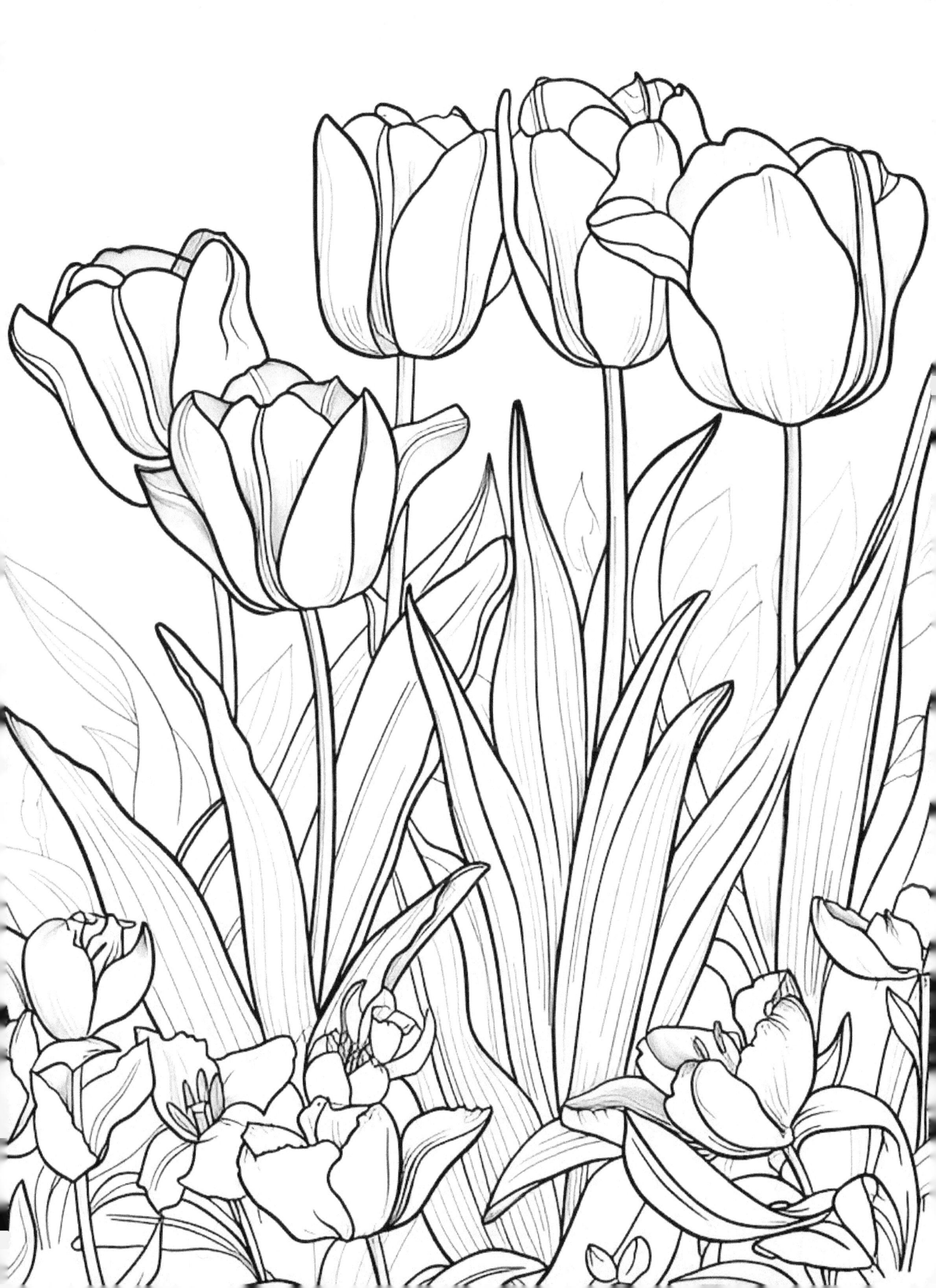

Tulips symbolize love, elegance and grace.

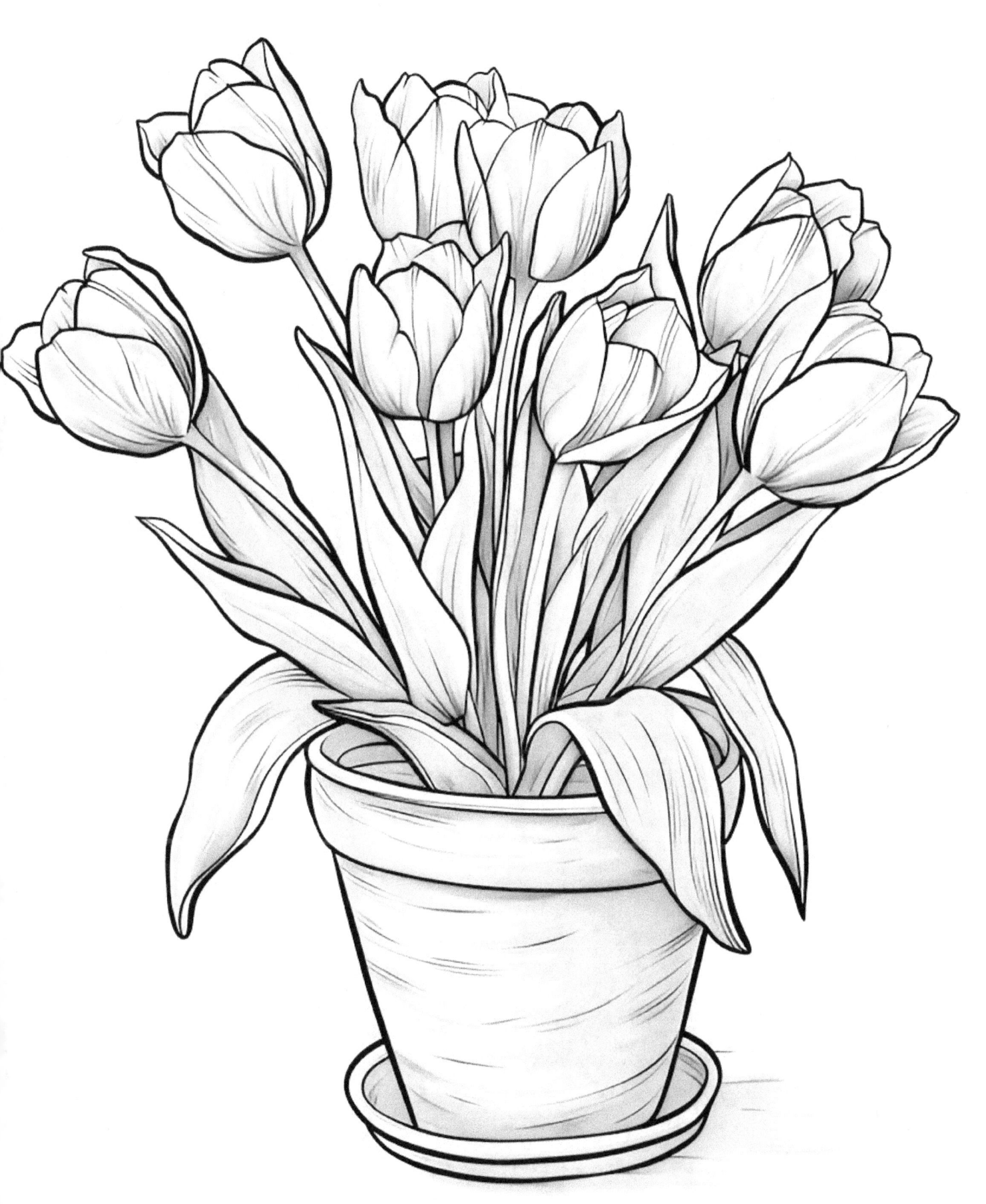

Tulips can grow in a wide range of climates and soil types.

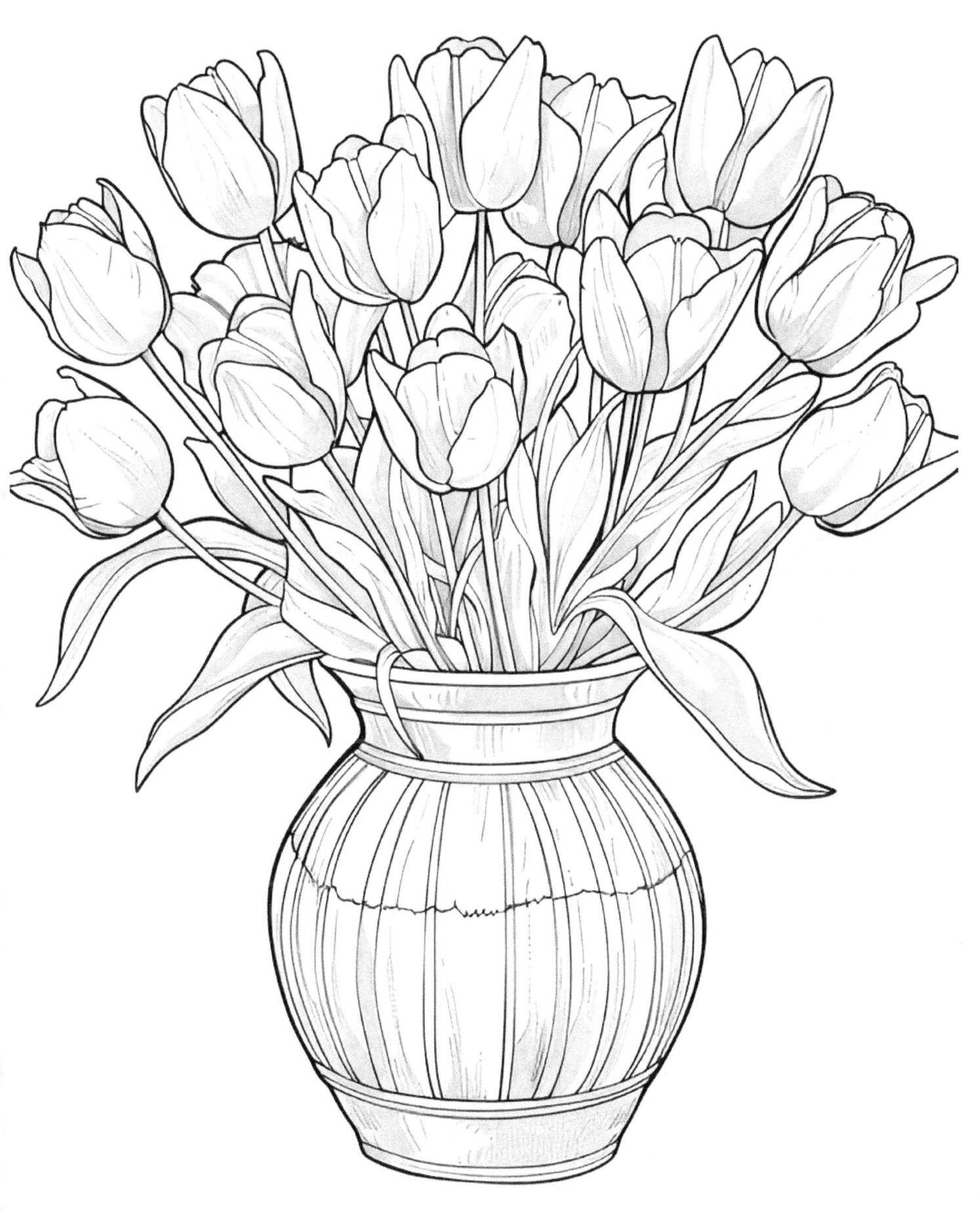

Tulips can be grown indoors as potted plants.

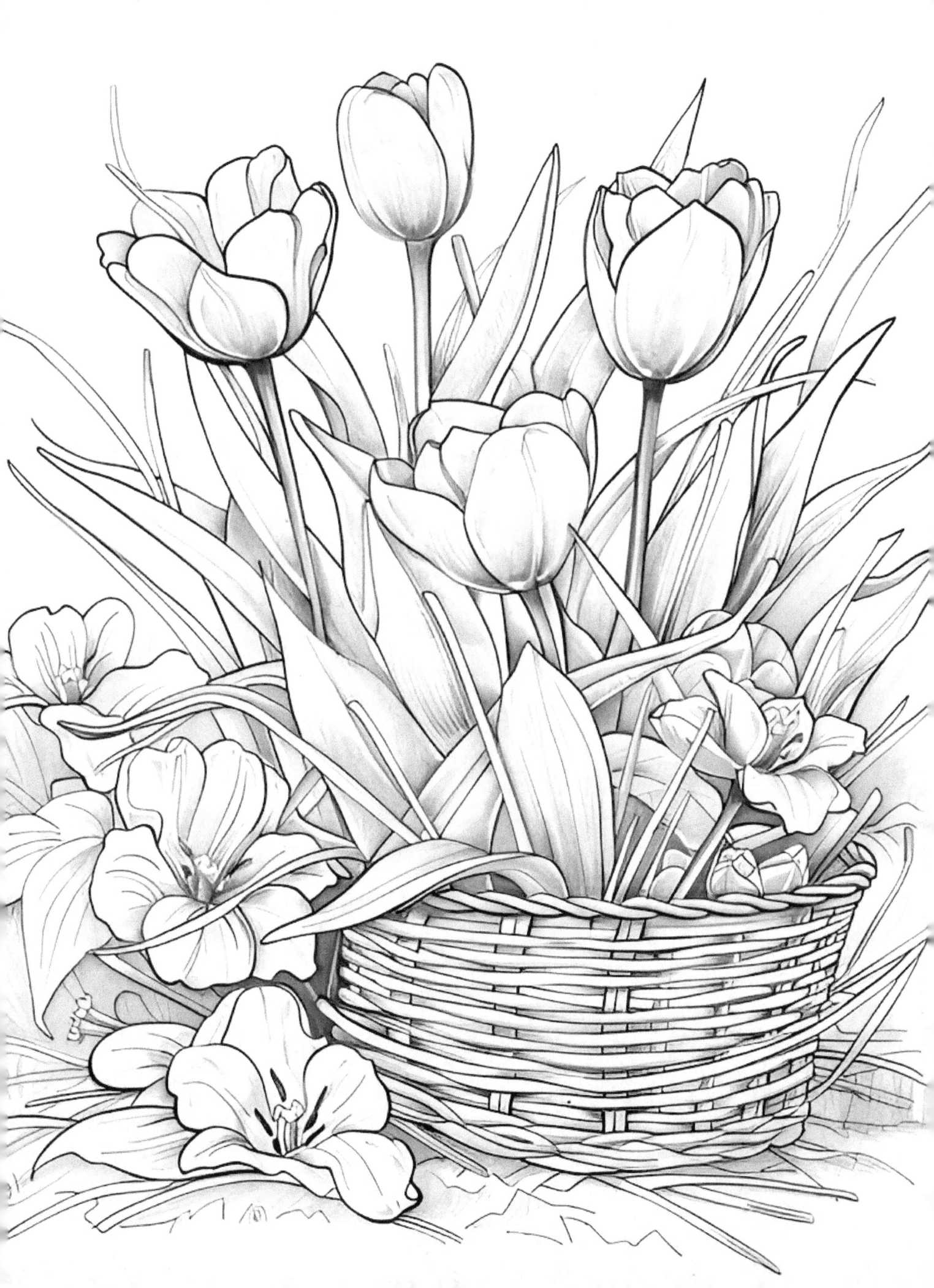

Tulips require well-drained soil and full sun to thrive.

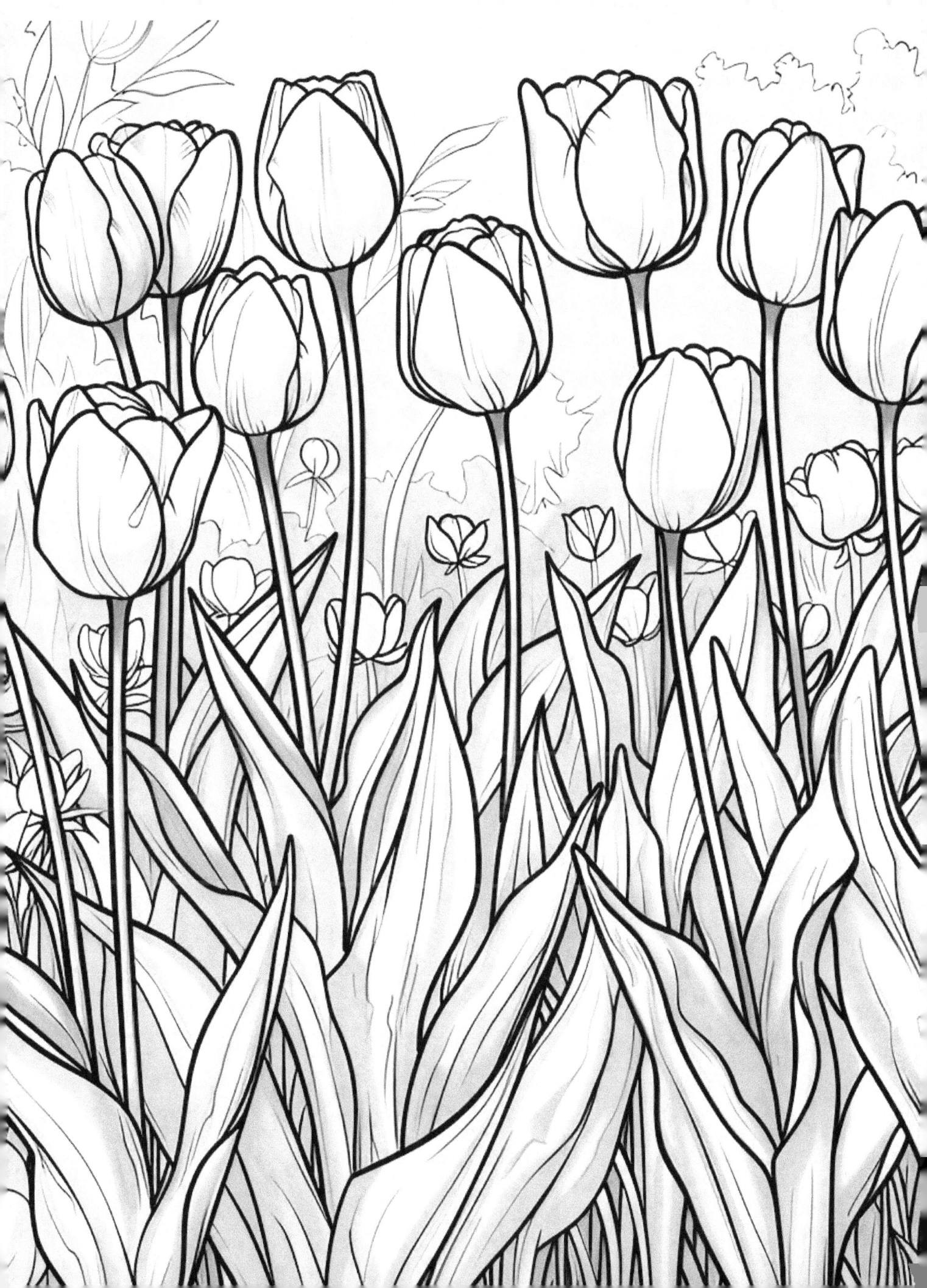

Tulips are often used as a symbol of spring and renewal.

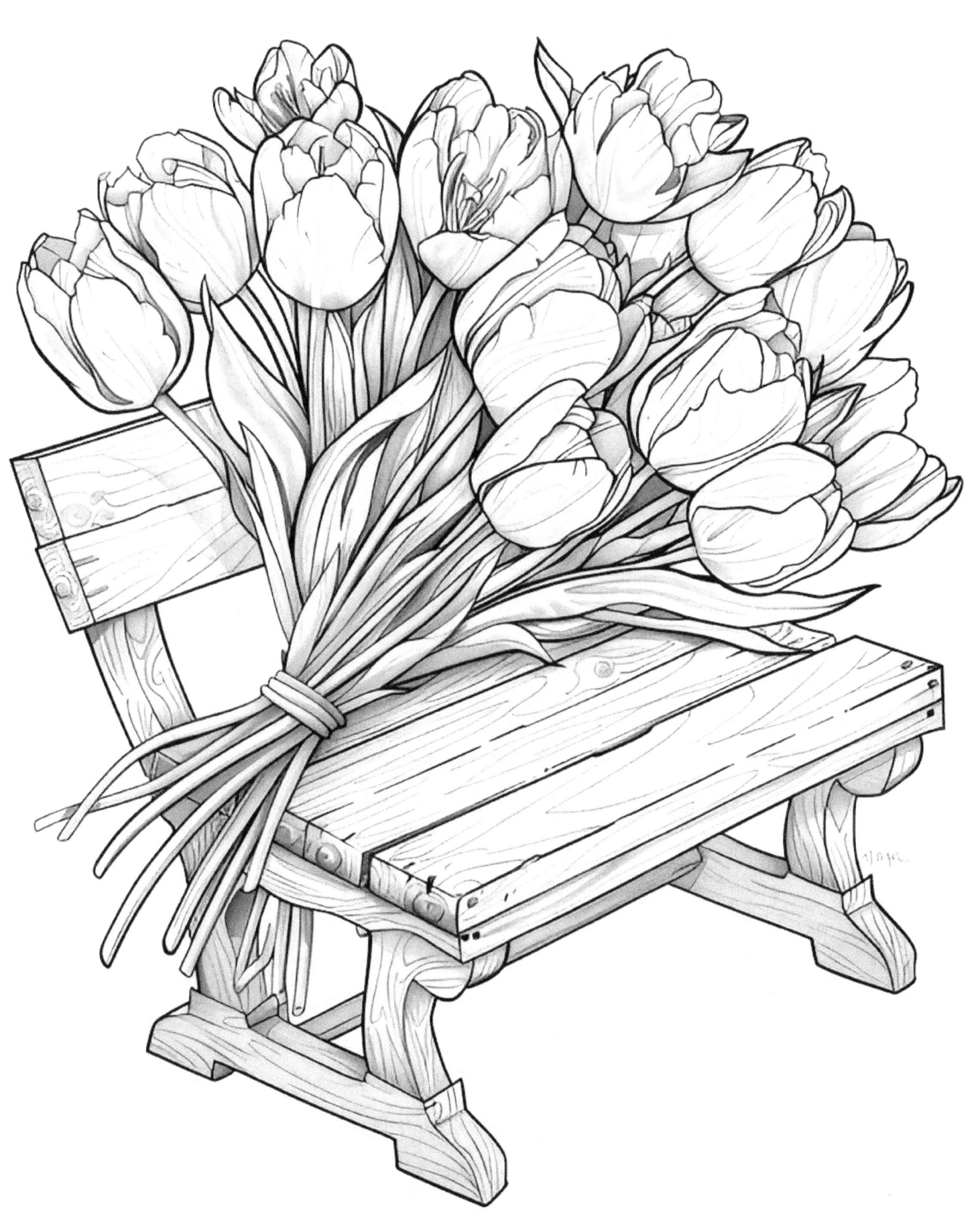

Tulips were first cultivated by the Ottoman Empire.

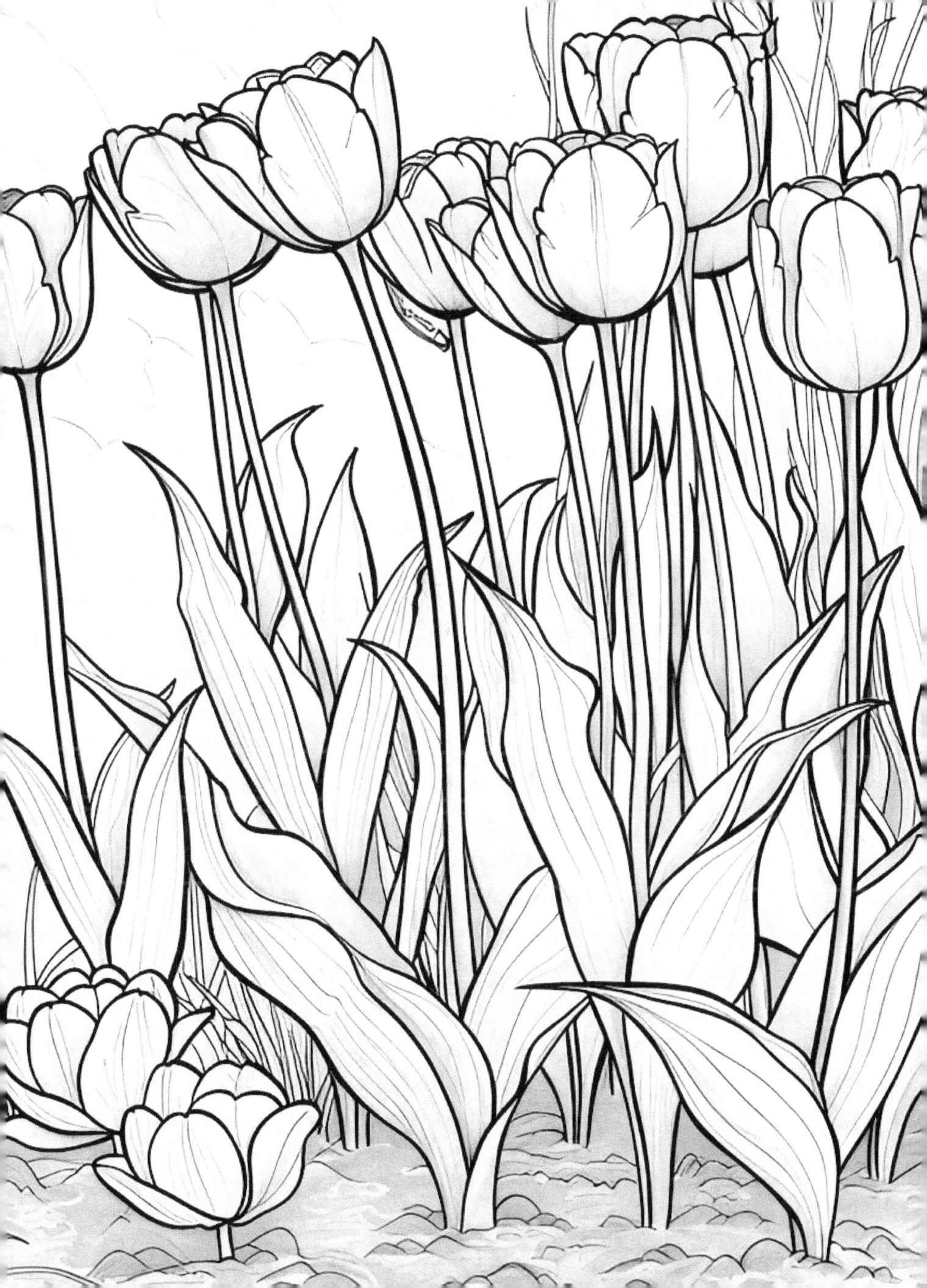

The Dutch "Tulip Festival" celebrates the flower's beauty every spring.

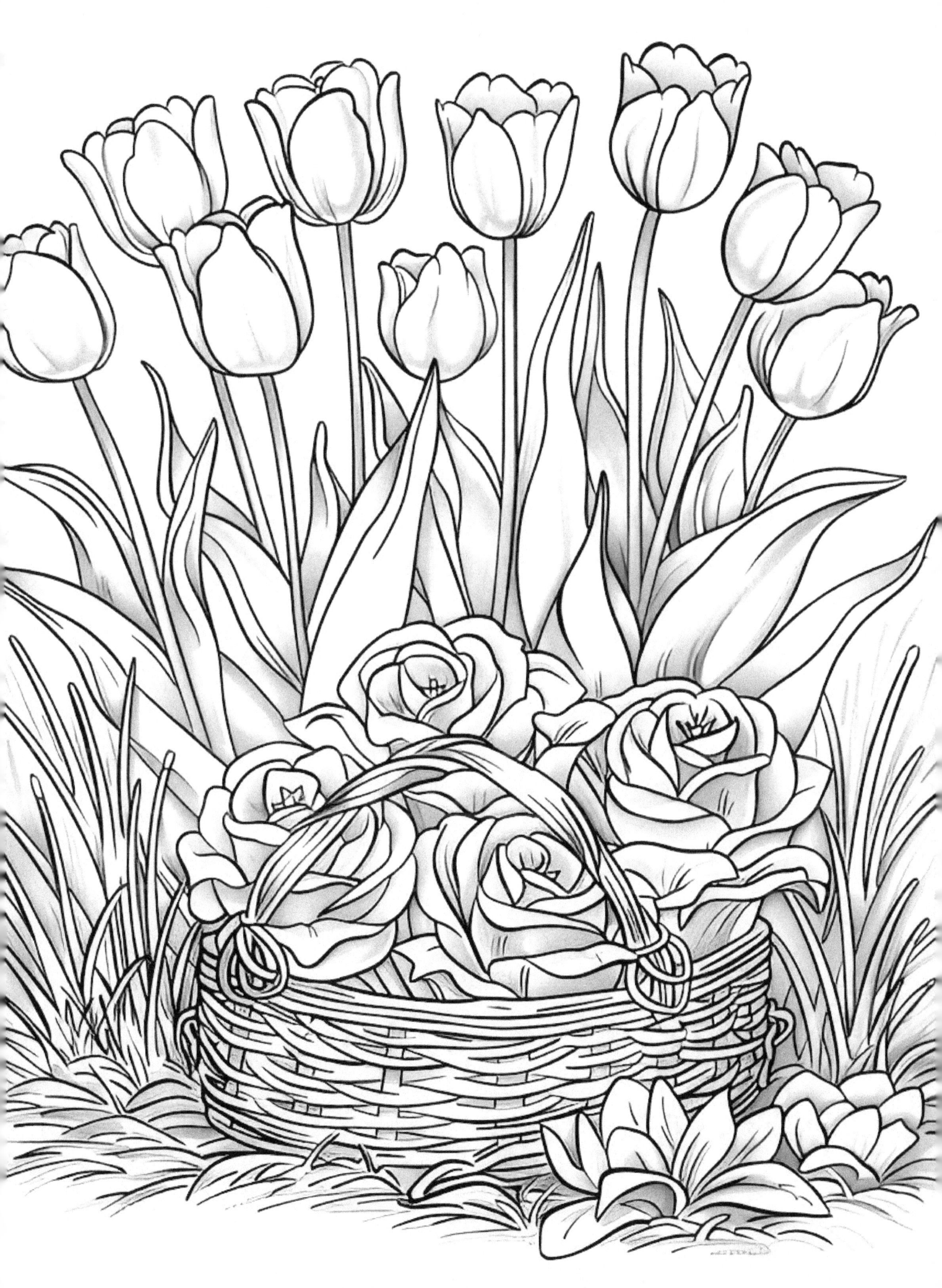

Tulips can be propagated through seeds, bulbs or offsets.

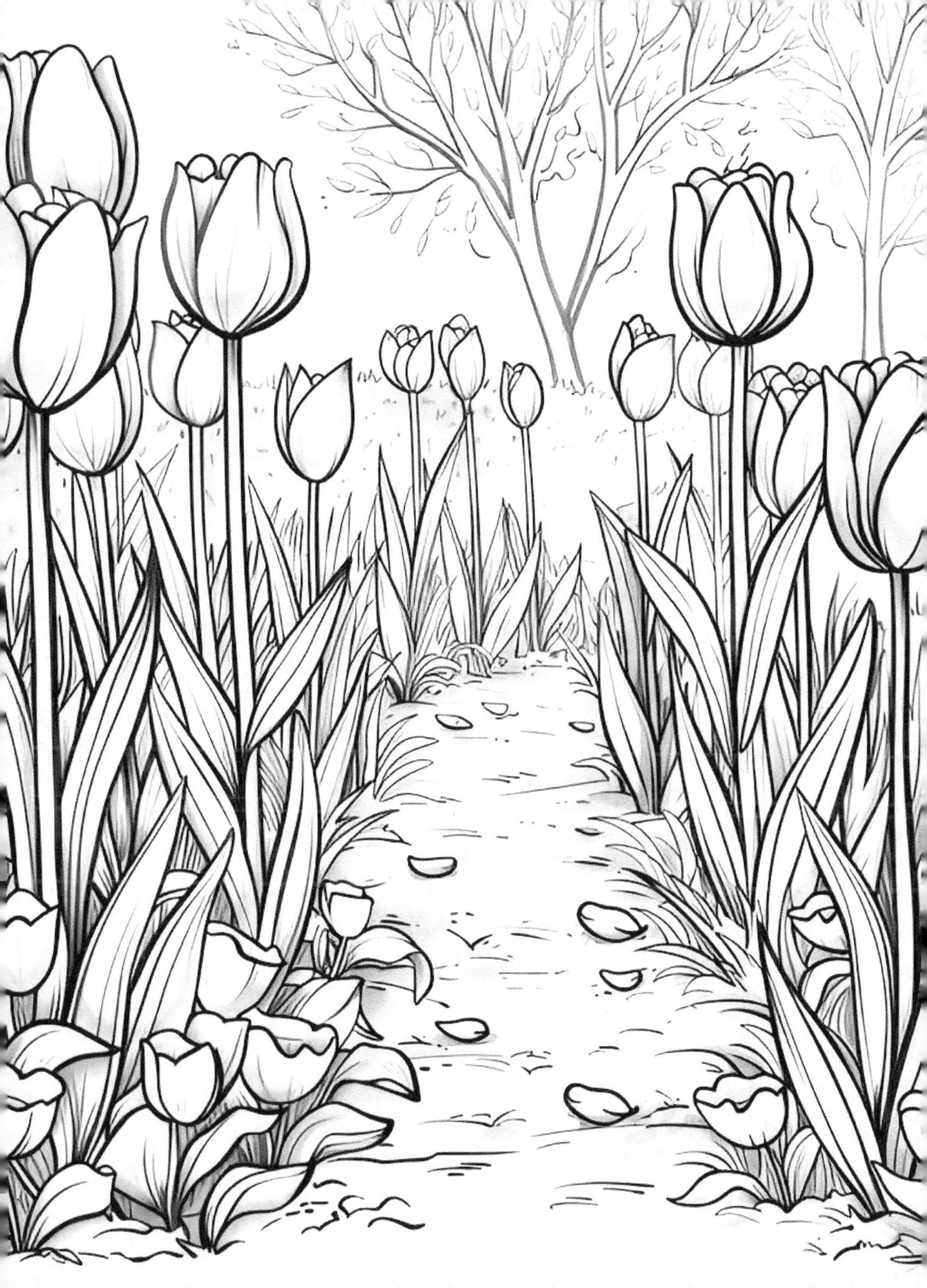

Tulpis were introduced to Europe by traders from Ottoman Empire.

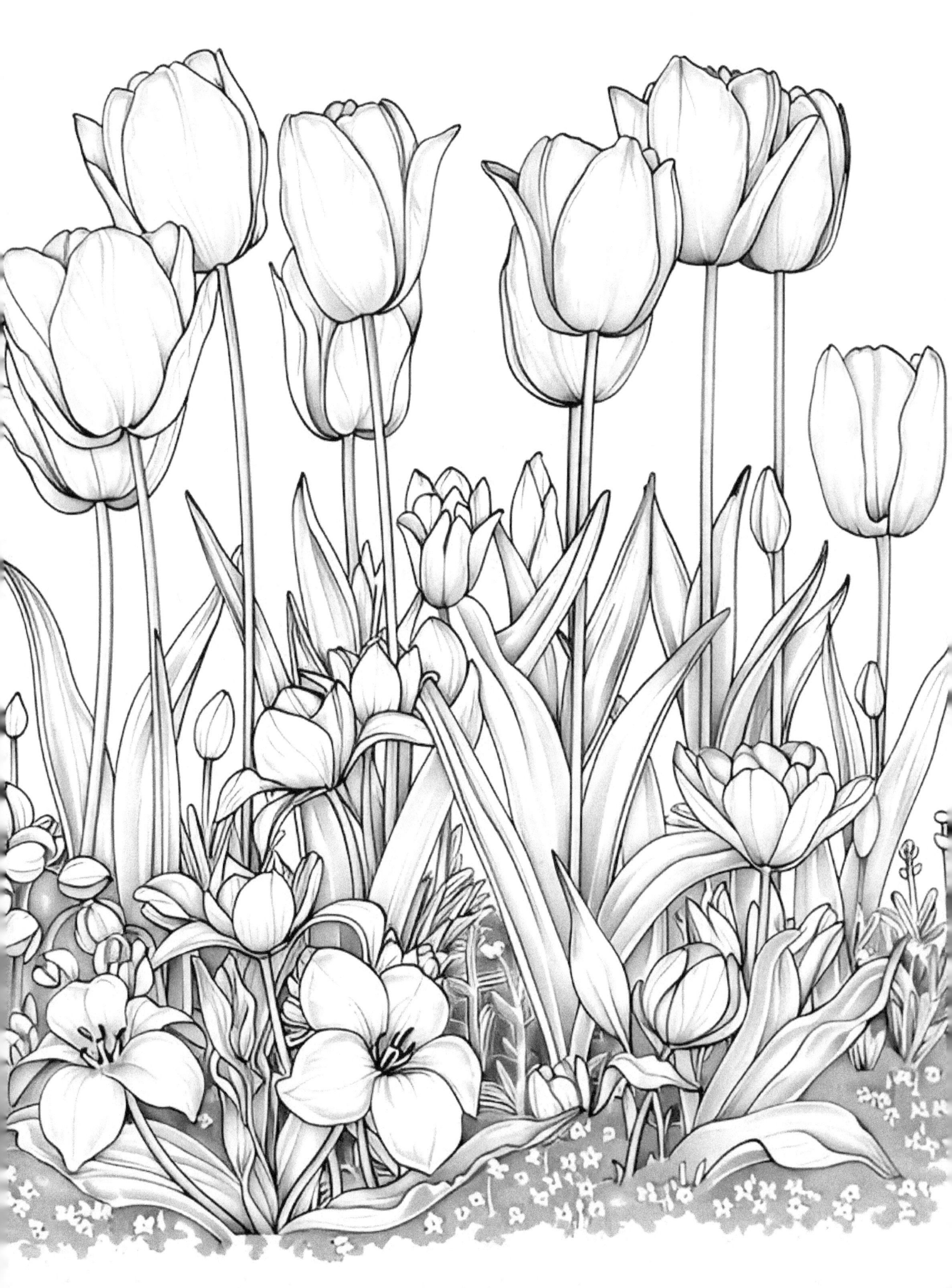

Tulips are one of the most popular flowers for gardens and landscapes.

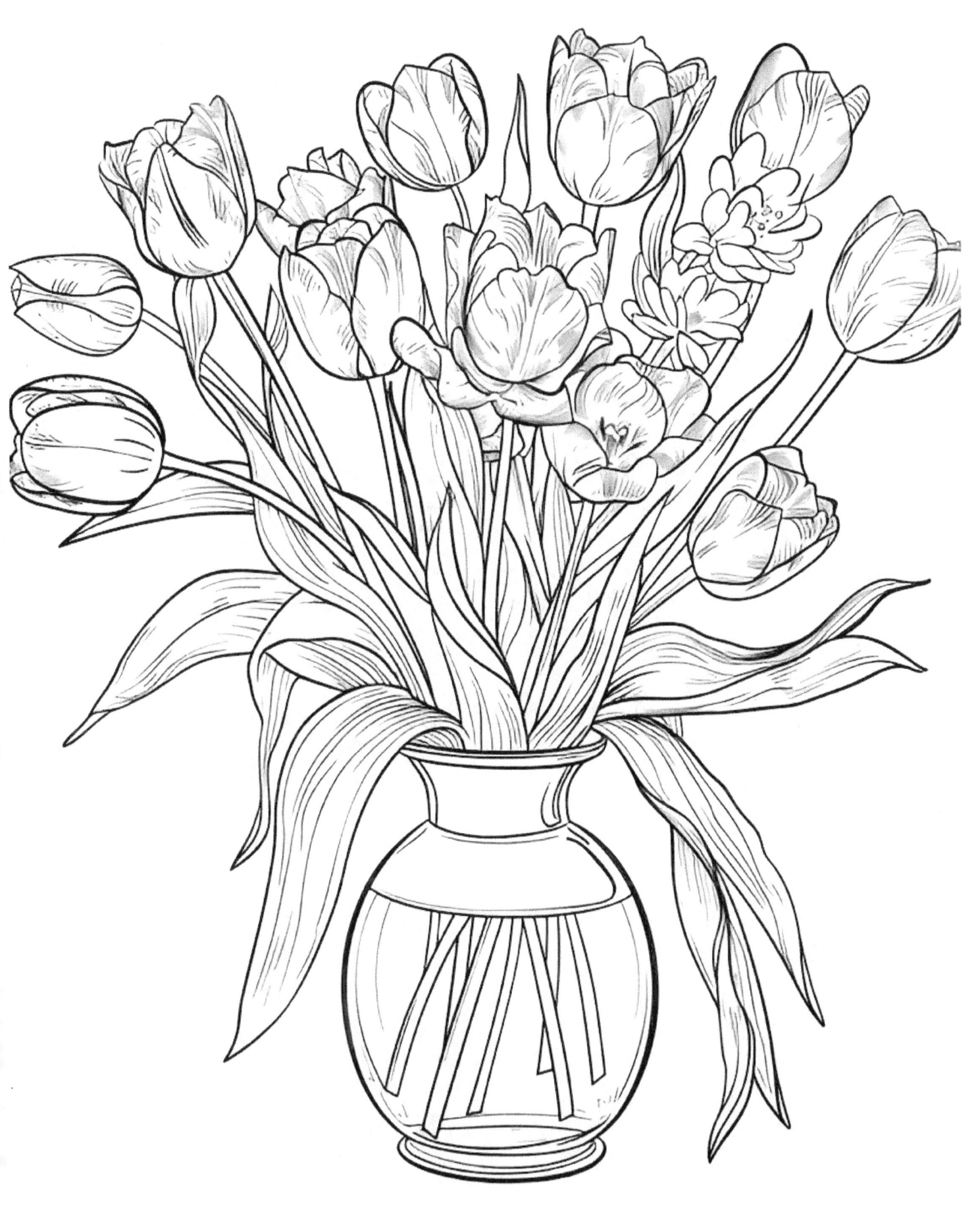

Tulips were used as a symbol of wealth prosperity in the Ottoman Empire.

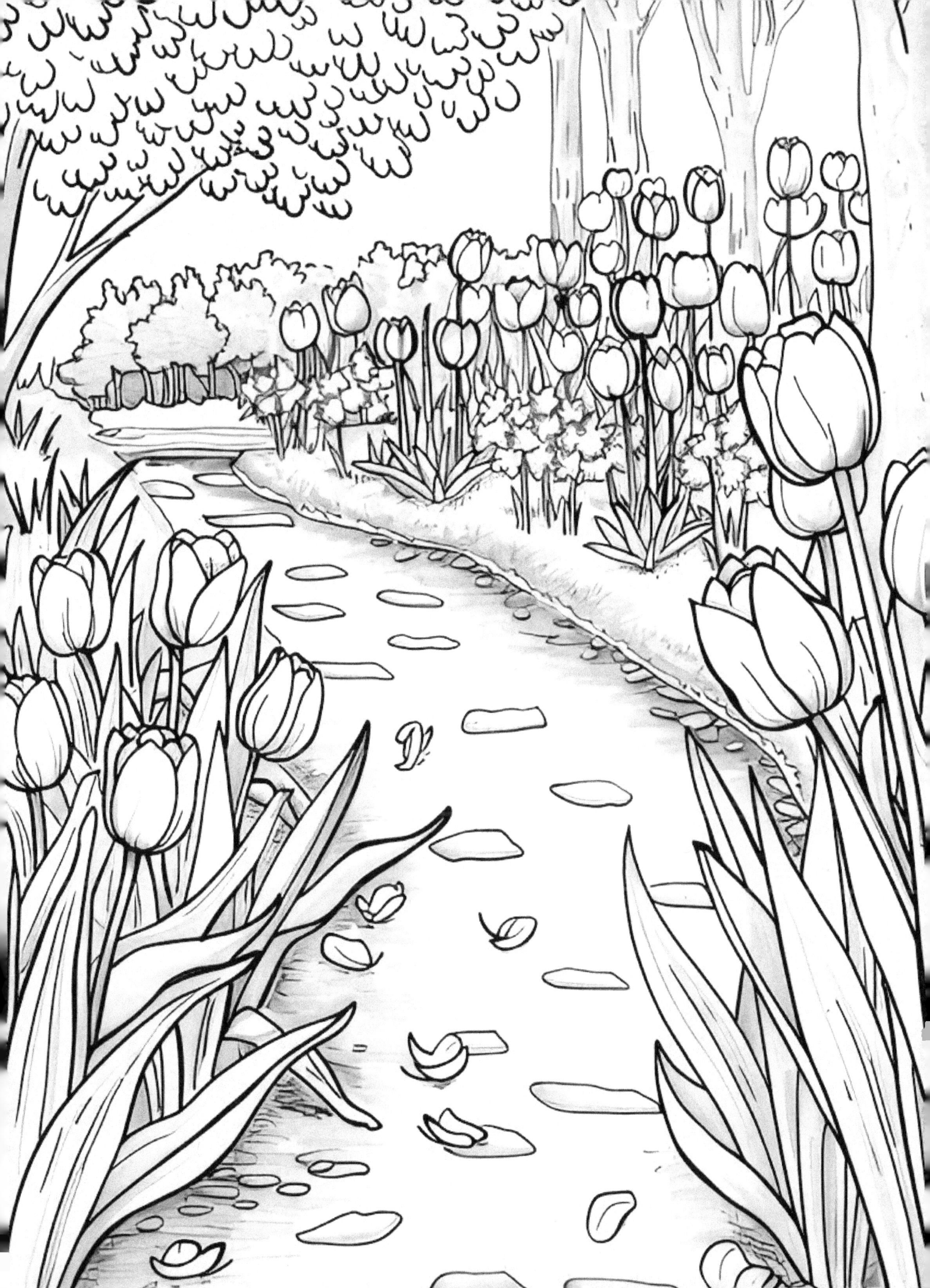

Tulips have a short blooming period, typically lasting 1-3 weeks.

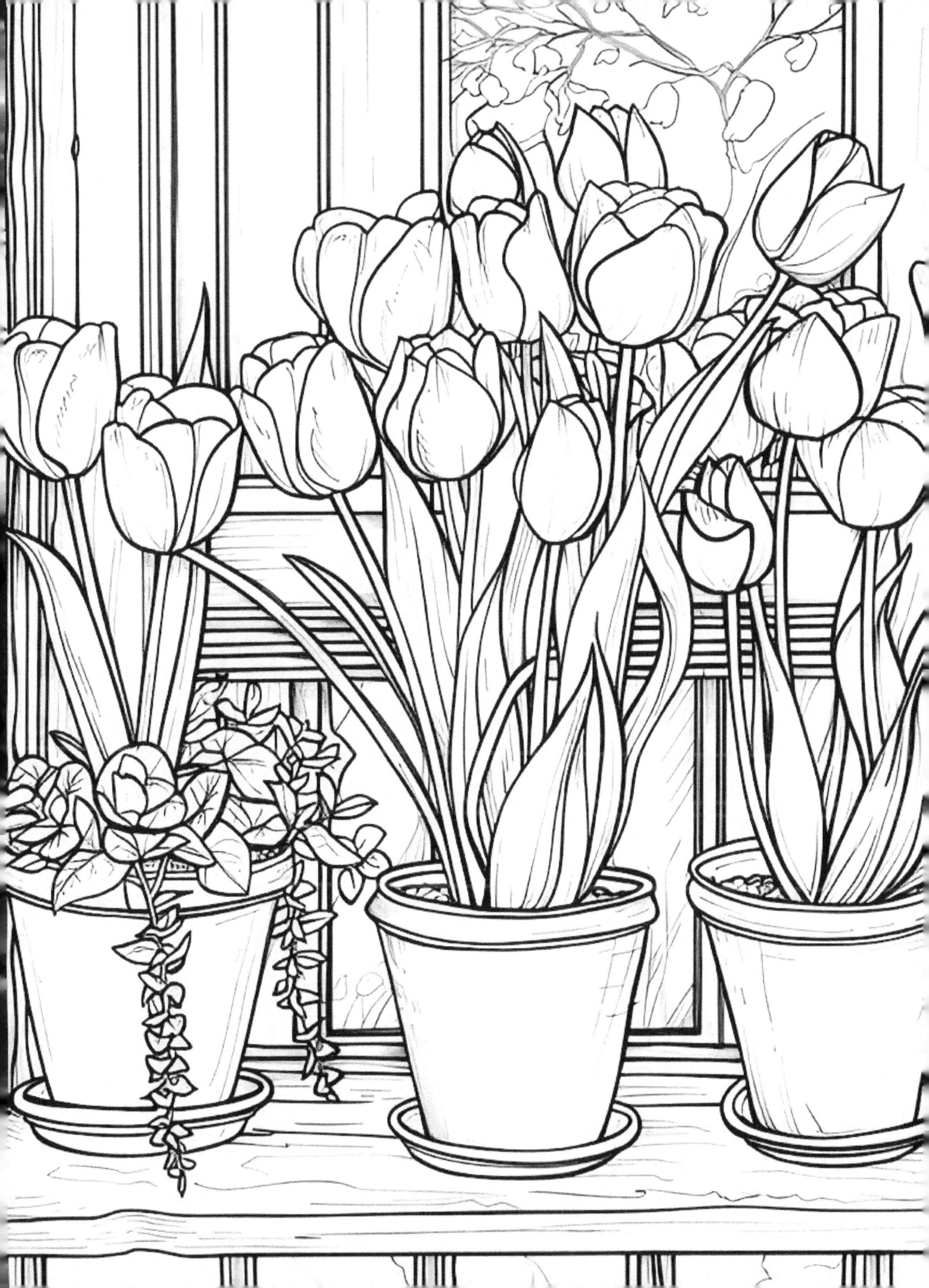

Tulips were once used as a form of currency in Turkey.

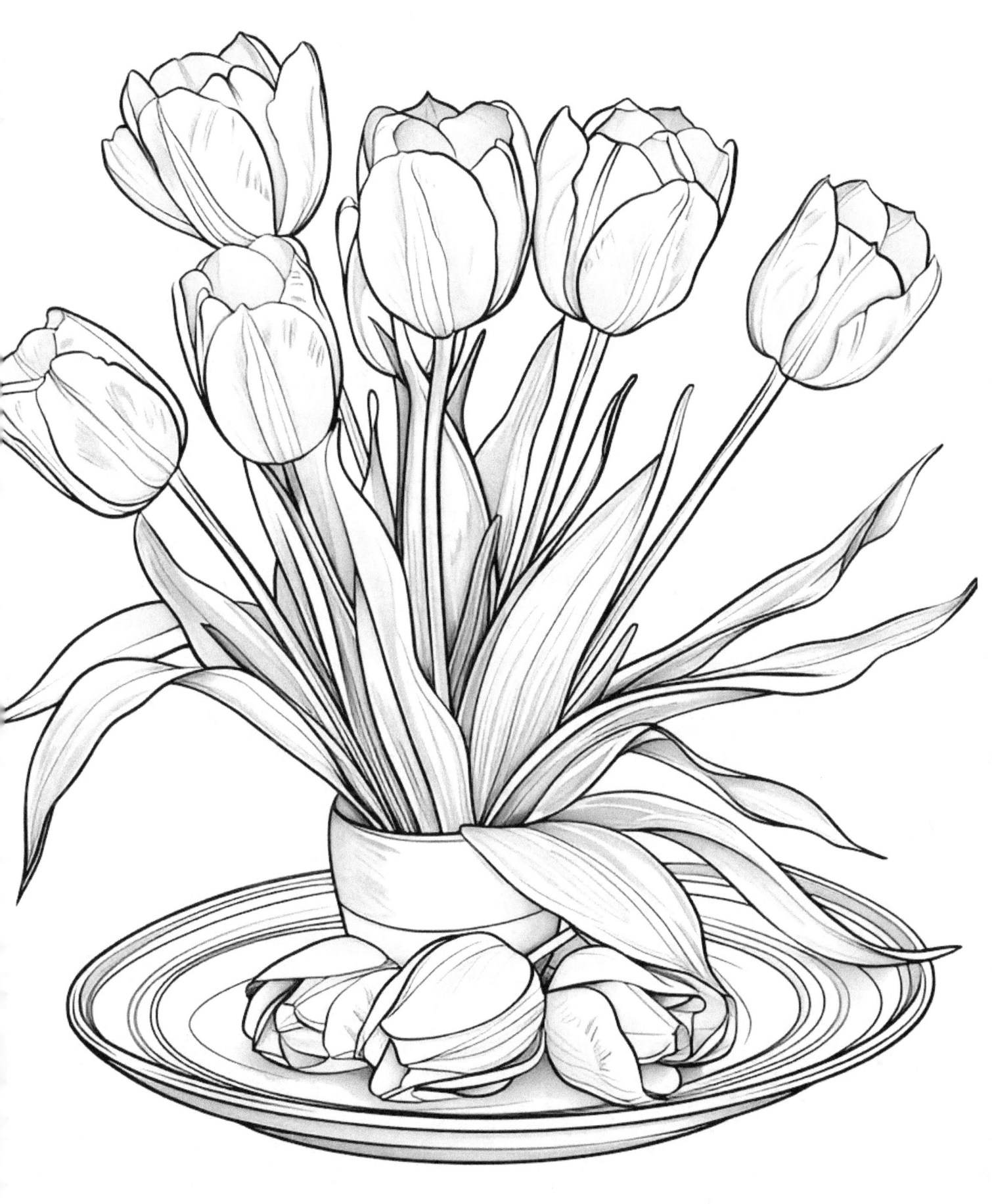

Tulips can be found in a wide range of color including red, pink, yellow, orange, purple and white.

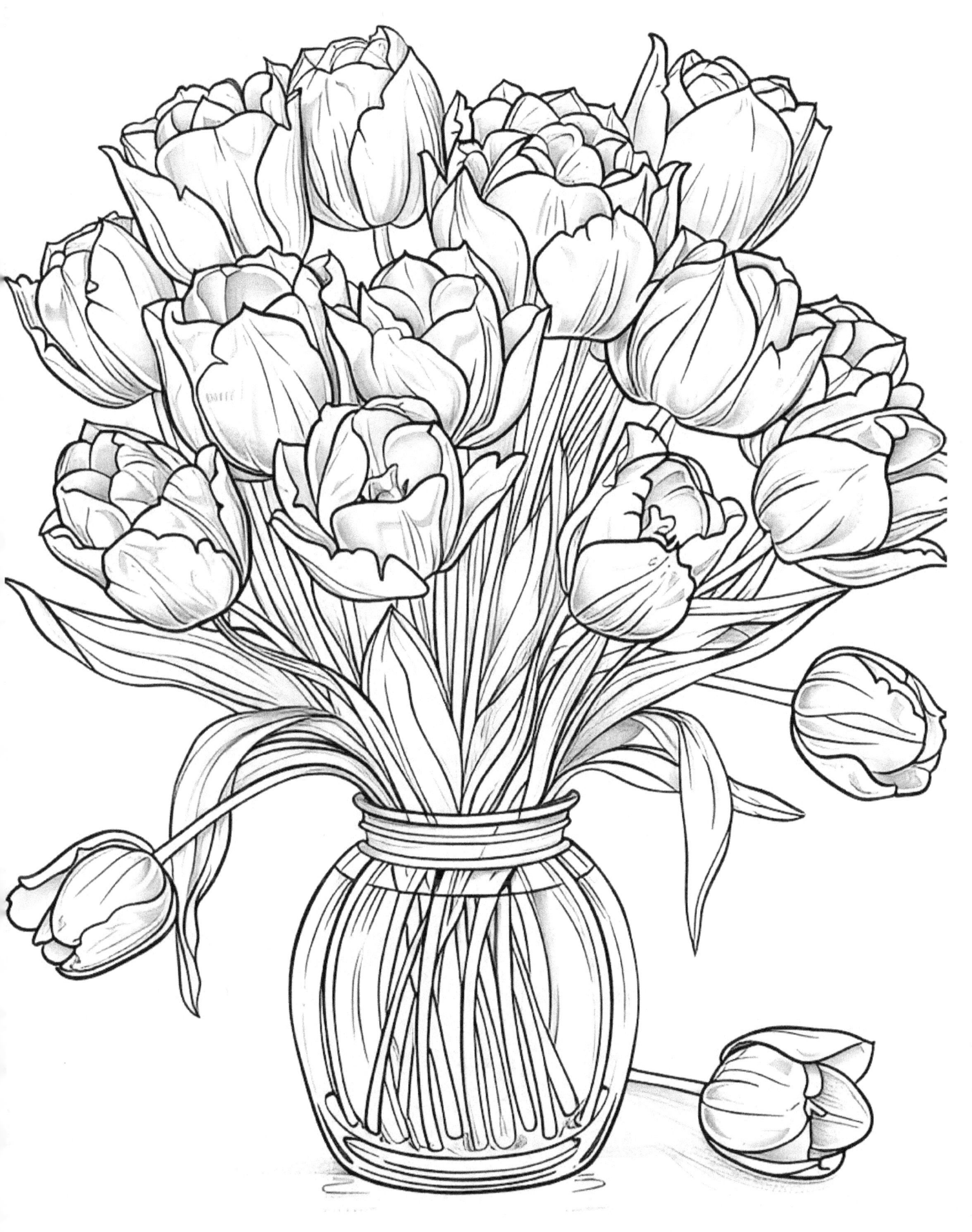

Tulips are susceptible to diseases such as tulip fire and tulip breaking virus.

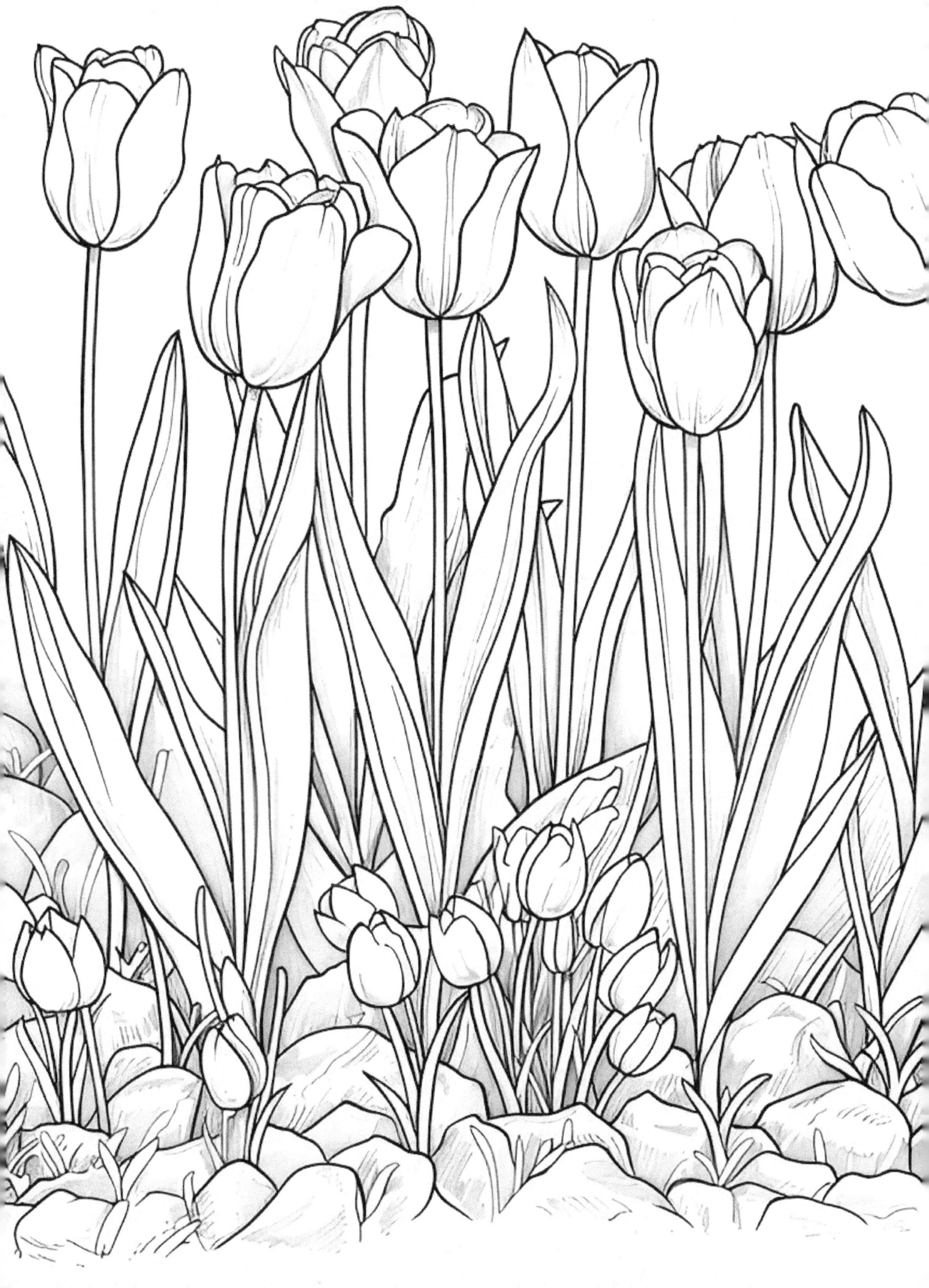

Tulips have been depicted in art and literature for centuries.

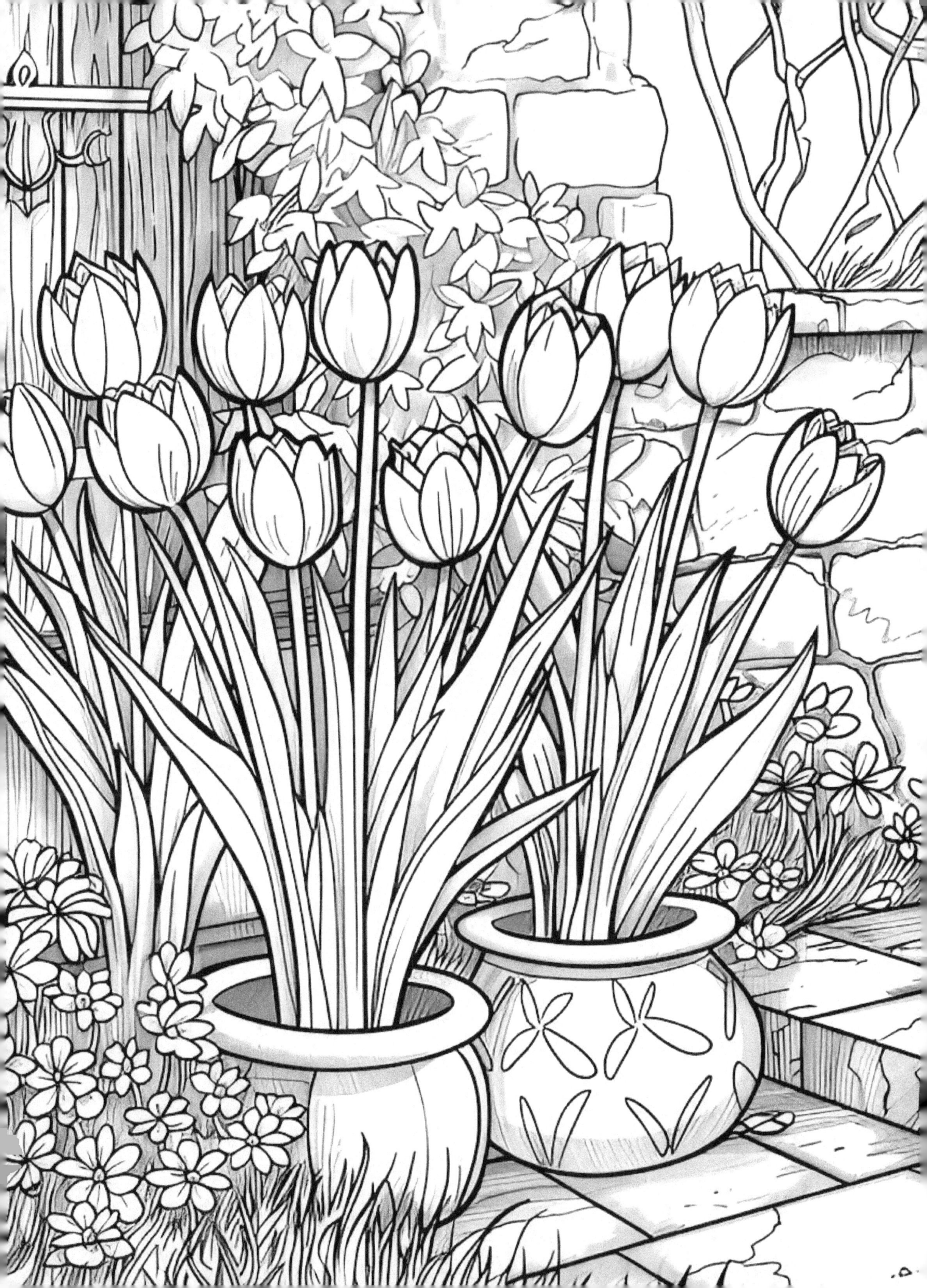

Tulip bulbs are planted in the fall and bloom in the spring.

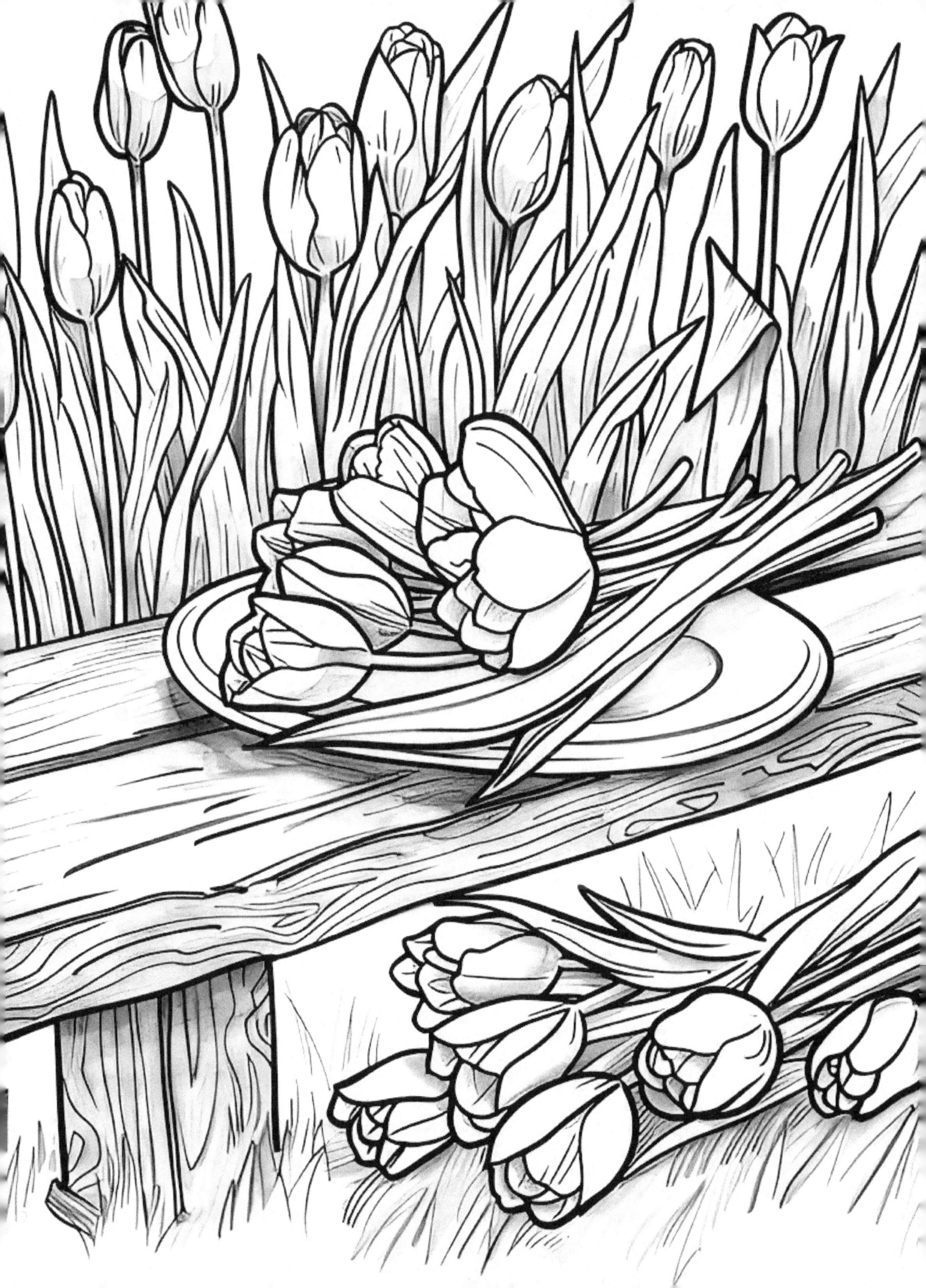

Tulips are often used to symbolize new beginnings and hope.

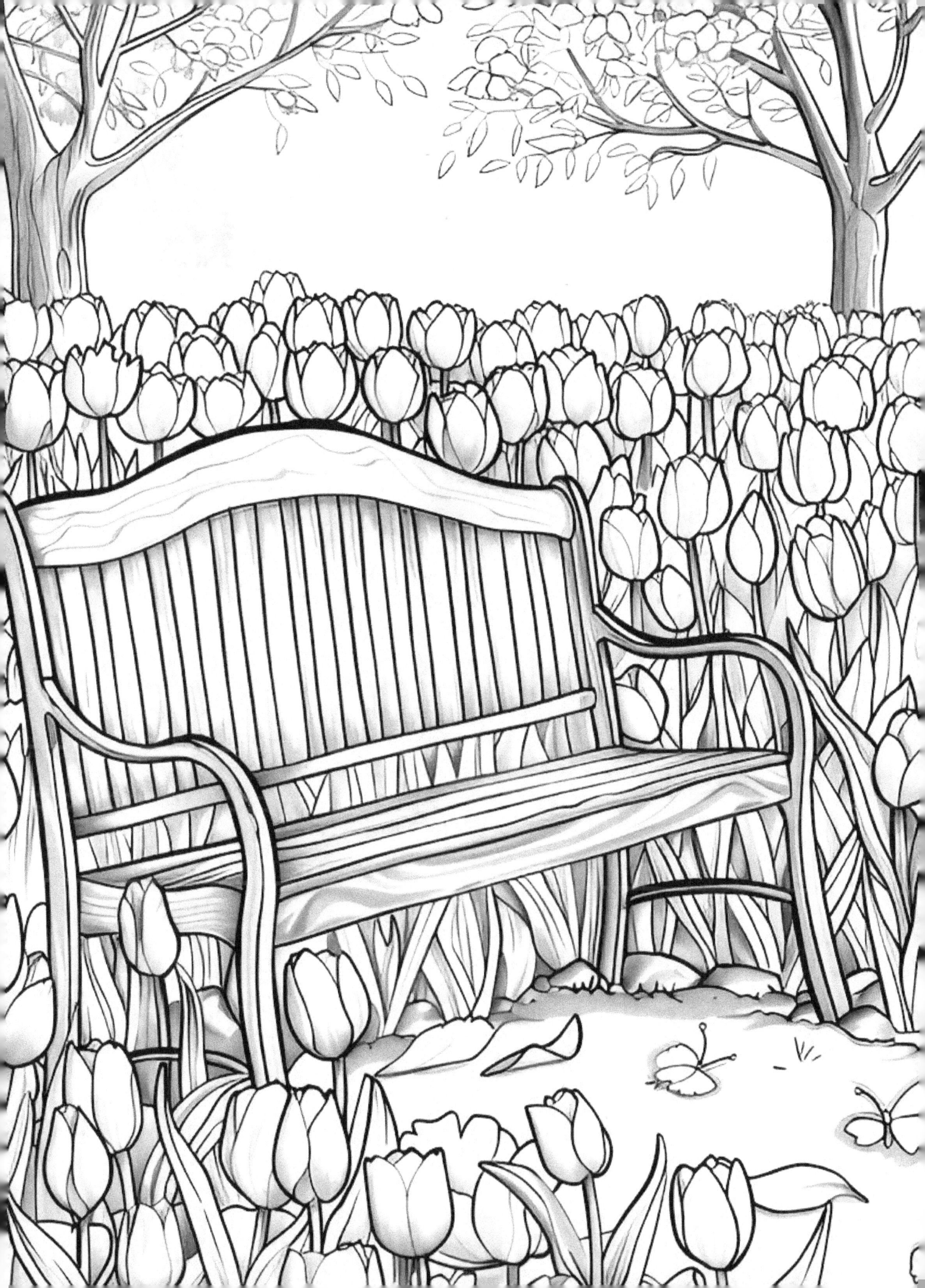

Tulips are often used in landscaping, borders and flowerbeds.

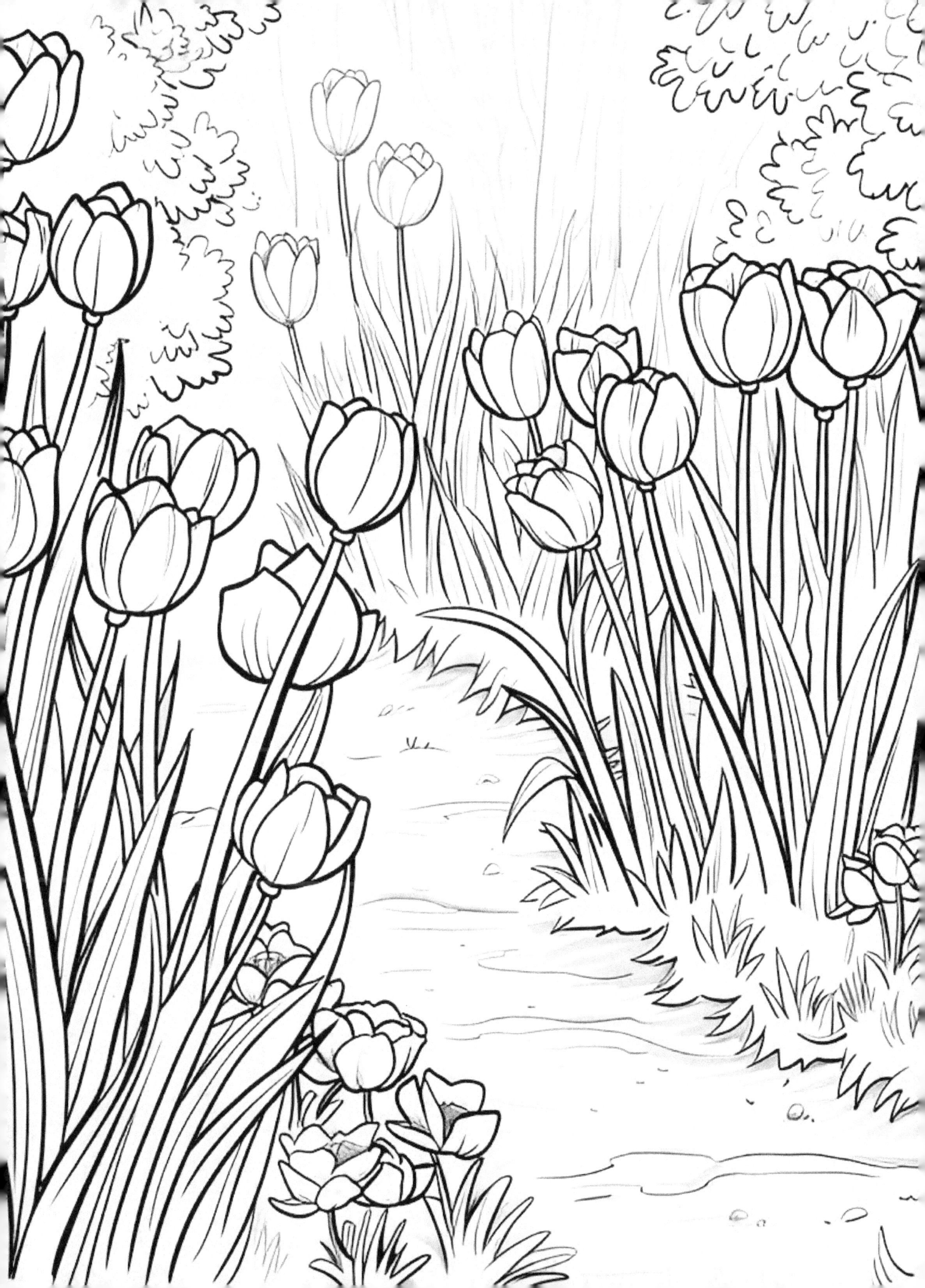

Tulips are known for their graceful and elegant appearance.

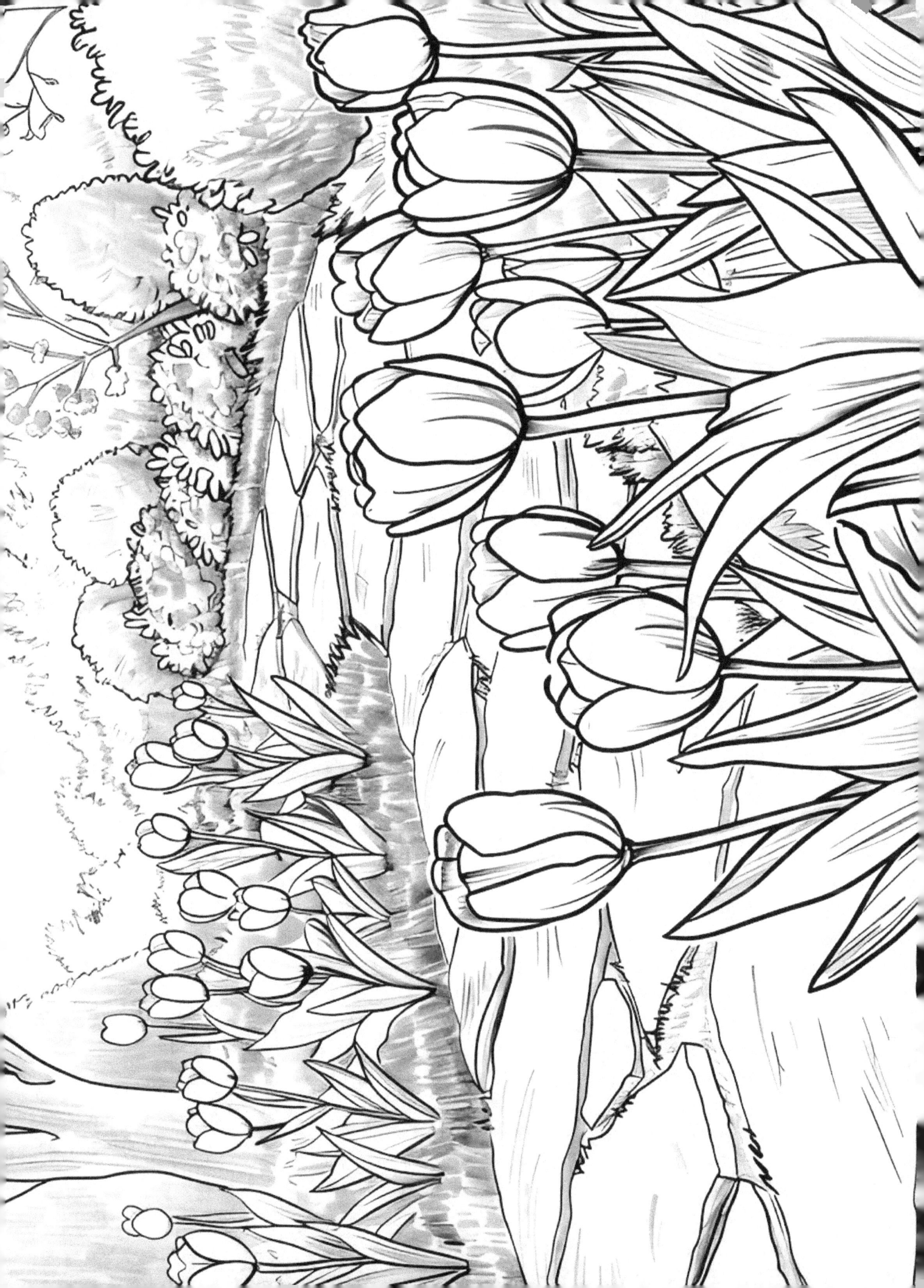

Tulips festivals are held in various countries around the world.

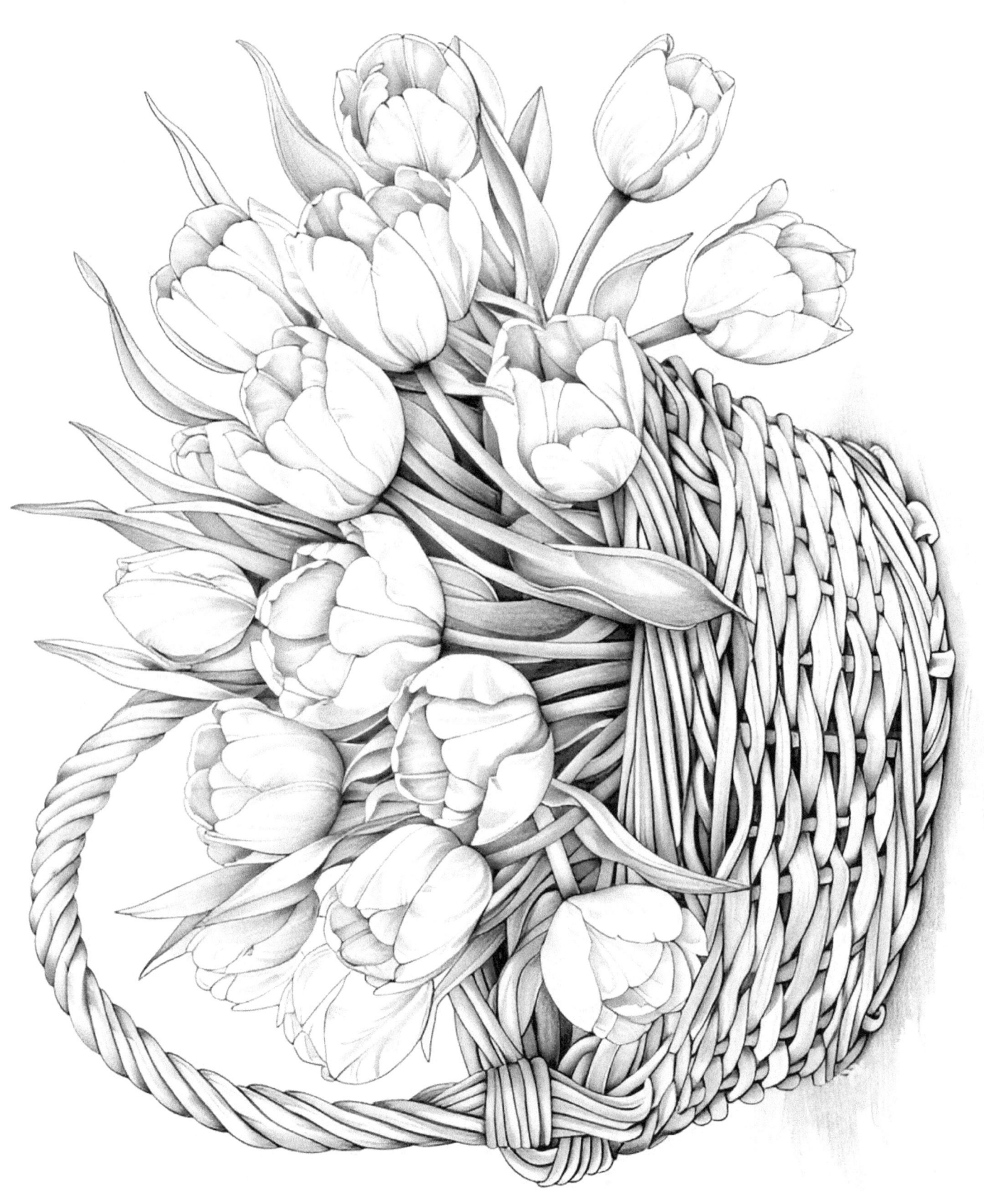

Tulips are often used as a cut flower in floral arrangements.

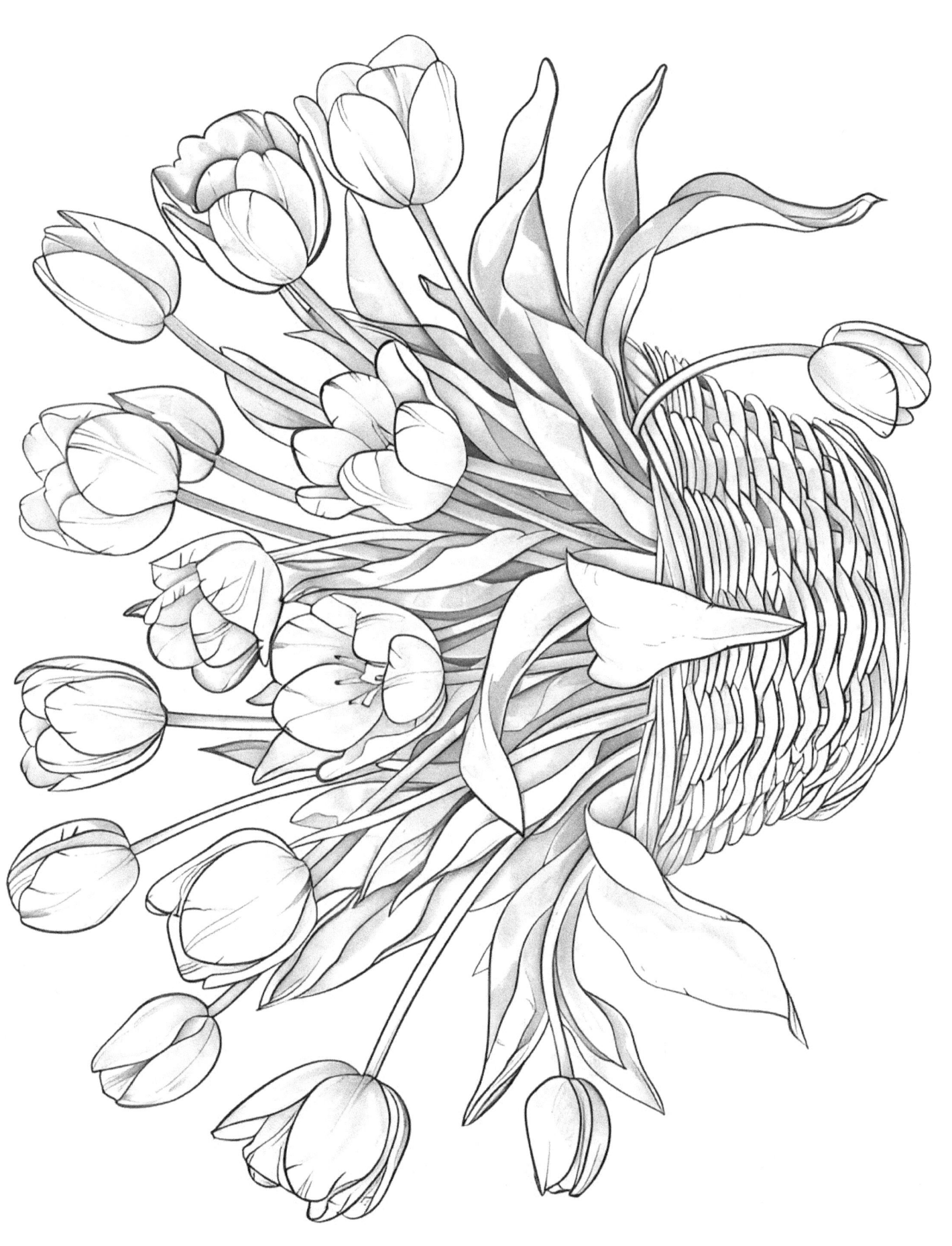

Tulips have been cultivated for centuries for their beauty and symbolism.

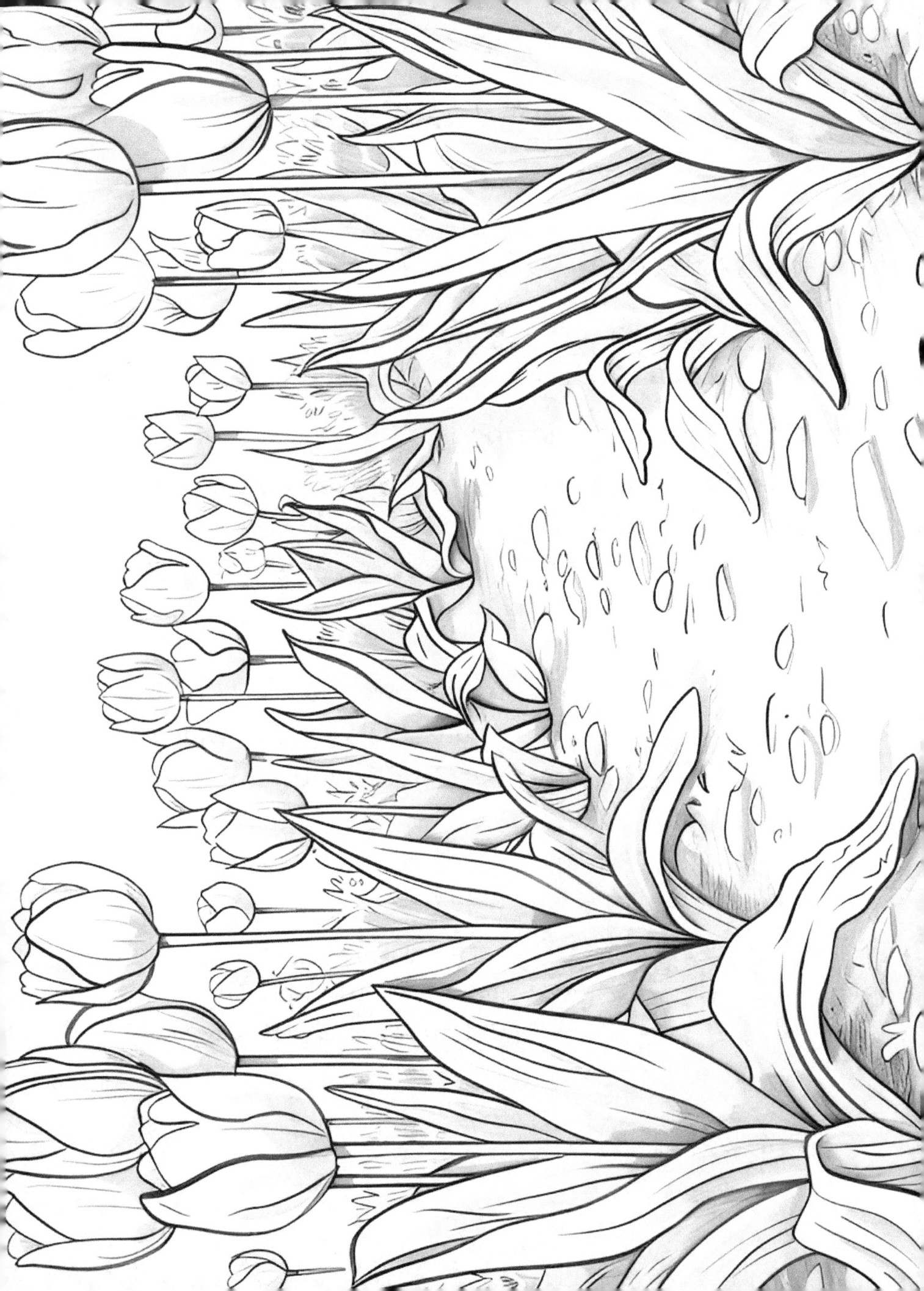

Liked it!
You can find more

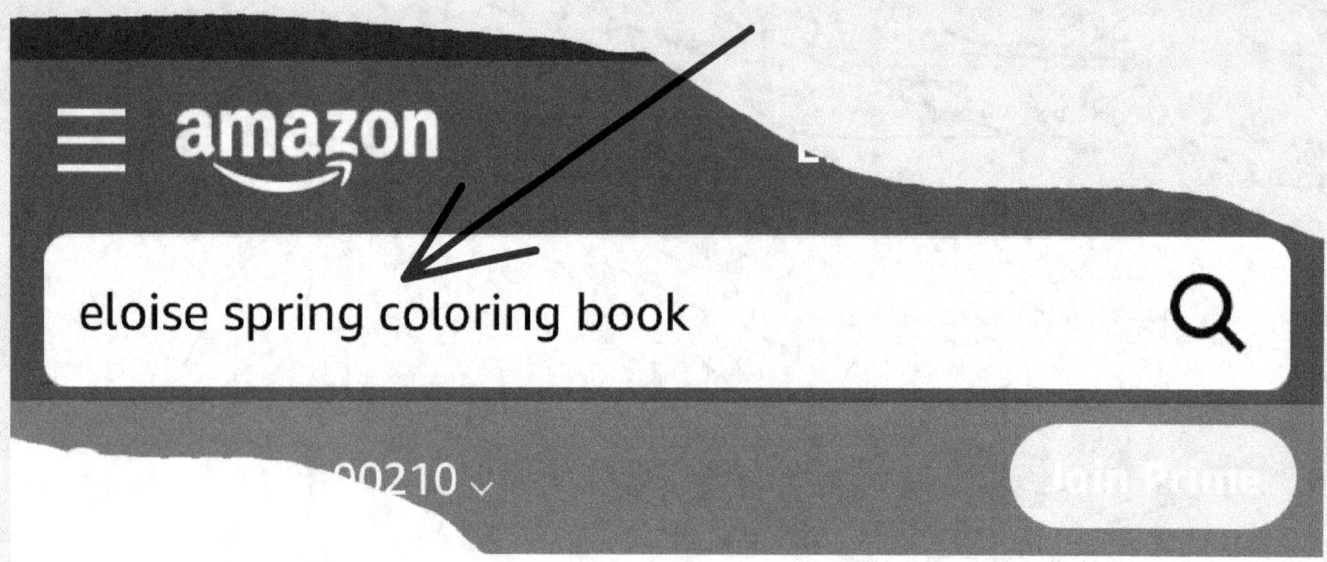

*If you find pleasure in bringing these pages to life, I would be delighted if you share your experiences and leave a review on Amazon.
Thank you.*

☆ ☆ ☆ ☆ ☆

© All rights Reserved.
No part of this publication may be reproduced, distributed or transmitted in any form or be any means, including photocopying, recording or other electronic or mechanical method, without prior written permission of the publisher, except in the case of brief quotation embodied in critical reviews and certain other noncommercial uses permitted by copyright law.

www.ingramcontent.com/pod-product-compliance
Lightning Source LLC
Chambersburg PA
CBHW082215220526
45470CB00010B/3177